# TOP **10**
# DELHI

GAVIN THOMAS
JANICE PARIAT

EYEWITNESS TRAVEL

Left **Detail, Jamali-Kamali Masjid** Centre **Park, Connaught Place** Right **Beating the Retreat**

LONDON, NEW YORK,
MELBOURNE, MUNICH AND DELHI
www.dk.com

Reproduced by Colourscan, Singapore
Printed and bound in China by Leo
Paper Products Ltd.

First published in Great Britain in 2010
by Dorling Kindersley Limited,
80 Strand, London, WC2R 0RL
A Penguin Company

**Copyright 2010 © Dorling
Kindersley Limited, London**

A CIP catalogue record is available from
the British Library

ISBN 978 1 4053 5168 3

Within each Top 10 list in this book, no
hierarchy of quality or popularity is
implied. All 10 are, in the editor's
opinion, of roughly equal merit.

MIX
Paper from
responsible sources
FSC
www.fsc.org   FSC™ C018179

# Contents

## Delhi's Top 10

| | |
|---|---|
| Highlights of Delhi | 6 |
| Red Fort | 8 |
| Chandni Chowk | 10 |
| Jama Masjid | 12 |
| Humayun's Tomb | 14 |
| Around Rajpath | 16 |
| Qutb Minar Complex | 18 |
| Crafts Museum | 22 |
| Lodi Gardens | 24 |
| National Museum | 26 |
| Taj Mahal, Agra | 30 |
| Moments in History | 36 |
| Cities of Delhi, Old and New | 38 |
| Festivals and Events | 40 |
| Delhi Sultanate Sights | 42 |
| Mughal Delhi Sights | 44 |
| Bazaars of Old Delhi | 46 |

**The information in this DK Eyewitness Top 10 Travel Guide is checked regularly.**
Every effort has been made to ensure that this book is as up-to-date as possible at the time of
going to press. Some details, however, such as telephone numbers, opening hours, prices,
gallery hanging arrangements and travel information are liable to change. The publishers
cannot accept responsibility for any consequences arising from the use of this book, nor for
any material on third party websites, and cannot guarantee that any website address in this
book will be a suitable source of travel information. We value the views and suggestions of
our readers very highly. Please write to: Publisher, DK Eyewitness Travel Guides,
Dorling Kindersley, 80 Strand, London WC2R 0RL.

Left **Street life in Old Delhi** Centre **Jantar Mantar** Right **Posters for sale in Chandni Chowk**

Monuments of the
1857 Uprising                        48

Performing Arts Venues               50

Places of Worship                    52

Museums and Galleries                54

Parks and Gardens                    56

Delhi-inspired Books                 58

Walks Around Delhi                   60

Shops and Markets                    62

Places to Eat                        64

Bars and Nightclubs                  66

Excursions from Delhi                68

**Around Town**

New Delhi                            72

Old Delhi                            80

South of the Centre                  88

South Delhi                          94

**Streetsmart**

Planning Your Trip                   104

Getting There and Around             105

Sources of Information               106

Practicalities                       107

Banking and
Communications                       108

Security and Health                  109

Things to Avoid                      110

Shopping Tips                        111

Accommodation Tips                   112

Dining and Drinking Tips             113

Places to Stay                       114

General Index                        120

Selected Street Index                128

Left **Humayun's Tomb** Right **Chatta Chowk at the entrance to the Red Fort**

*Key to abbreviations*
**Adm** *admission*

# DELHI'S TOP 10

Highlights of Delhi
6–7

Red Fort
8–9

Chandni Chowk
10–11

Jama Masjid
12–13

Humayun's Tomb
14–15

Around Rajpath
16–17

Qutb Minar Complex
18–21

Crafts Museum
22–23

Lodi Gardens
24–25

National Museum
26–29

Taj Mahal, Agra
30–33

Top 10 of Everything
36–69

DELHI'S TOP 10

# 🔟 Highlights of Delhi

*History is writ large in Delhi, and few other places in the world can rival the city's incredible glut of monuments, spanning 1,000 years of Indian history. These range from the soaring medieval minaret of the Qutb Minar to world-famous Mughal monuments such as the Red Fort, the dramatic Jama Masjid and Humayun's Tomb, as well as some of the most grandiose Imperial landmarks of the British Raj, such as Rajpath, India Gate and Rashtrapati Bhavan.*

### Red Fort

Former residence of the all-powerful Mughal emperors, the enormous Red Fort is Old Delhi's showpiece attraction, providing a fascinating glimpse into the opulent and cultured world of the country's most charismatic rulers *(see pp8–9)*.

### Chandni Chowk

At the heart of Old Delhi, this famous Mughal thoroughfare offers a colourful slice of quintessential Indian street life, lined with mosques, temples and myriad shops, thronged with a constant melee of shoppers and sightseers *(see pp10–11)*.

### Jama Masjid

The largest and most spectacular mosque in India, this superb Mughal monument rises dramatically out of the labyrinthine streets of Old Delhi *(see pp12–13)*.

### Humayun's Tomb

The first of the great Mughal garden tombs, this is one of the most beautiful, and biggest, of all Delhi's ancient monuments *(see pp14–15)*.

### Rajpath

The centrepiece of Imperial Delhi, this great Raj-era thoroughfare is one of the world's finest examples of Colonial pomp, stretching from the stately India Gate to the grand Rashtrapati Bhavan *(see pp16–17)*.

Deer Park

Hauz Khas Village

GAMAL ABDEL NASSER MG

SHAHEED JEET SINGH MG

AUROBINDO MARG

Sanjay Van

PRESS ENCLAVE MARG

6

MEHRAULI BADARPUR RD

1000 ⌐ yards ⌐ 0 ⌐ meters

Preceding pages **Interior courtyard of the Jama Masjid**

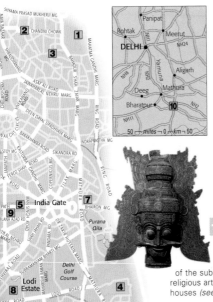

### Qutb Minar Complex
Towering over southern Delhi, the Qutb Minar is perhaps the city's single most dramatic sight, surrounded by many monuments dating from the Sultanate and Mughal periods *(see pp18–21)*.

### Crafts Museum
This engaging museum offers a fascinating snapshot of the myriad local arts-and-crafts traditions of the subcontinent, from arcane religious artifacts to traditional village houses *(see pp22–3)*.

### Lodi Gardens
The idyllic Lodi Gardens are dotted with a sequence of atmospheric tombs built in honour of the Delhi sultans. The landscaped grounds make it perfect for a picnic *(see pp24–5)*.

### National Museum
The National Museum is India's finest, with an enormous collection of artifacts and exhibits ranging from the Harappan civilization to the 20th century, covering every aspect of the country's wonderfully varied cultural history *(see pp26–9)*.

### Taj Mahal
Perhaps the most famous – and certainly the most beautiful – building in the world, the incomparable Taj Mahal in Agra never fails to astonish and amaze, whether one is seeing it for the first or the 50th time *(see pp30–31)*.

# TOP 10 Red Fort

*In 1638, the Mughal Emperor Shah Jahan (r.1628–58) decided to leave Agra, then capital of the empire, and return to Delhi. Here he created Shahjahanabad, or Old Delhi as it is now known, with the Red Fort (Lal Qila) at its heart. The fort was completed in 1648 and served as home to the emperor and his successors until the 1857 Uprising (see pp36–7). Although time has taken its toll on the place, the fort remains one of Delhi's most absorbing sights, offering a glimpse into the opulent lifestyle of the city's former rulers.*

*Pietra dura detail in the Diwan-i-Aam*

🕐 Arrive early to avoid the crowds and long entrance queues.

☕ The attractive Dawat Khana café at the far end of the Hayat Bakhsh Bagh is a good place for a drink. There is also a more down-at-heel café near the entrance to the fort.

• Map H3
• Chandni Chowk
• Chandni Chowk Metro
• Open Tue–Sun sunrise–sunset
• Rs.250 (Indian citizens Rs.10)
• Video Rs.25

## Top 10 Features

1. The Walls
2. Lahori Gate
3. Hayat Bakhsh Bagh
4. Naqqar Khana
5. Diwan-i-Aam (Hall of Public Audience)
6. Rang Mahal
7. Moti Masjid
8. Khas Mahal
9. Diwan-i-Khas (Hall of Private Audience)
10. Shah Burj and Burj-i-Shamali

### The Walls
Enormous red sandstone walls surround the complex, stretching 2.5 km (1.5 miles) and reaching a height of 30 m (98 ft) in places. Their intense colour lends the fort its name.

### Lahori Gate
Entrance to the fort is via the majestic Lahori Gate, although its original grandeur has been obscured by the defensive bastion added by Mughal Emperor Aurangzeb (1618–1707), designed to force would-be attackers into a sideways approach.

### Hayat Bakhsh Bagh
North of the Moti Masjid is the Hayat Bakhsh Bagh (Life-Bestowing Gardens), with two small marble pavilions at either end, and the pretty Zafar Mahal *(above)*, a pleasure palace, in the middle of a pool.

### Naqqar Khana
The second of the fort's major gateways, the Naqqar Khana *(above)* marked the point at which visitors were obliged to dismount from their elephants, while musicians once performed from the gallery upstairs.

*There is a sound and light show (in English and Hindi) at the Red Fort. Call ahead for timings on 2328 1802 or 2327 4580.*

**Diwan-i-Aam**
One of the fort's most impressive structures, this elegant sandstone pavilion *(above)* is where the emperor used to hold his public audiences.

**Rang Mahal**
The centre of the fort's women's quarters *(below)* has delicately carved marble walls and the remains of intricate mirrorwork on the ceiling.

**Moti Masjid**
Built in 1659, the Moti Masjid is closed to visitors, though it is possible to peer through its latticed marble screens for a glimpse of the delicate courtyard within.

**Khas Mahal**
The emperor's lavishly decorated private apartments *(below)* are divided in two by a lattice screen surmounted by the scales of justice.

**Diwan-i-Khas**
This pillared hall is where the emperor would have conferred with his ministers on affairs of state, and was also where Shah Jahan's legendary, jewel-encrusted Peacock Throne was formerly housed. It remains easily the most lavish building in the fort, with fine marble carving and pietra dura inlaywork.

**Shah Burj and Burj-i-Shamali**
The Shah Burj is where water was drawn from the Yamuna River for use in the fort. Aurangzeb subsequently added a fine marble pavilion, the Burj-i-Shamali, complete with a waterchute.

**The Fort in the Age of the Mughals**

Impressive as it is, what you see of the Red Fort today is only a part of the original structure – once a veritable city within a city, with pavilions and courtyards, many of which have now vanished. Much of the blame falls on the British, who, following the 1857 Uprising, razed many of the fort's buildings to the ground. They erected an overbearing sequence of barracks in their place which – unfortunately – survive to this day.

# TOP 10 Chandni Chowk

*When Shah Jahan built his new city, Chandni Chowk was planned as its principal thoroughfare – a broad, ceremonial avenue leading directly from the Red Fort and a favoured spot for elaborate processions. Most of the street's original buildings are now gone (along with the canal which ran down the middle of the road), but Chandni Chowk retains much of its traditional atmosphere, lined with shoebox shops, and eternally bustling with crowds and traffic.*

*Courtyard of the Sunehri Masjid*

🕊 The pavements of Chandni Chowk are busy and congested. A rickshaw ride along the road is a fun way to experience the scene without constantly having to watch one's step.

🍴 Halfway down Chandni Chowk is Haldiram's, a clean and efficient restaurant that serves a good variety of drinks, snacks and light meals.

- Map G3
- Chandni Chowk Metro

## Top 10 Features

1. Lal Mandir
2. Gauri Shankar Mandir
3. Begum Samru's Palace
4. Central Baptist Church
5. Gurudwara Sisganj
6. Lala Chunna Mal's Haveli
7. Sunehri Masjid
8. Town Hall
9. Sikh Museum (Bhai Mati Das Bhai Sati Das Bhai Dyala Museum)
10. Fatehpuri Masjid

### 1 Lal Mandir

Built during the reign of Shah Jahan for the Jain soldiers in his army, the Lal Mandir (Red Temple) *(below)* is one of Delhi's principal Jain shrines. Made of red Kota stone (hence the name) the temple's towers provide a major landmark at the fort end of Chandni Chowk.

### 2 Gauri Shankar Mandir

This vibrant Hindu temple, built for Shankar (Shiva) and Gauri (his wife Parvati), has an ancient *lingam*, a symbol of worship of the god Shiva, said to be 800 years old.

### 3 Begum Samru's Palace

Half-buried in the middle of a crowded bazaar just off the main street, this huge Neo-Classical mansion (now occupied by the Central Bank of India), was once one of the grandest buildings in Delhi, built in 1823, and surrounded by gardens which stretched all the way to Chandni Chowk.

### 4 Central Baptist Church

The first Christian mission in northern India when it was founded in 1814 (though the current building dates from 1858), the modest Central Baptist Church offers an atmospheric little memento of Raj-era Delhi.

*Chandni Chowk is also home to the famous Paranthe-wali Gully, the perfect place to snack on tasty paranthas see p85.*

### Gurudwara Sisganj

This large modern Sikh temple *(left)* commemorates the historic spot where the ninth Sikh guru, Teg Bahadur, was beheaded on the orders of Mughal Emperor Aurangzeb in 1675.

### Lala Chunna Mal's Haveli

Built by Hindu merchant Lala Chunna Mal in the wake of the 1857 Uprising, this sprawling, balconied mansion *(below)* has no less than 120 rooms.

### Sunehri Masjid

Small Mughal mosque (1721), named for its three gilded domes (*sunehri* meaning "golden"). It was from here that Persian invader Nadir Shah watched his soldiers massacre the city's inhabitants in 1739.

### Sikh Museum

This museum provides a comprehensive history of the Sikhs in pictures, including portraits of the ten Sikh gurus.

### Town Hall

The elegant British Town Hall, built in 1864, preserves a rather aristocratic air amidst the cluttered buildings of Chandni Chowk.

### Fatehpuri Masjid

Located at the west end of Chandni Chowk, the Fatehpuri Masjid *(below)* was built by a wife of Shah Jahan in 1650, and has an enormous and wonderfully peaceful courtyard.

### Ghantewala

Halfway down Chandni Chowk is Ghantewala, the oldest sweet shop in Delhi, established in 1790 and still owned by the original founding family. Renowned for its *laddoos* and *sohan halwa* (a Delhi speciality, made from dry fruits), the shop's name means "the one who rings the bell" in tribute to an emperor's elephant, who turned up at the shop one day jangling his bells and refusing to move until he had been fed.

# 🔟 Jama Masjid

*Completed in 1656, the Jama Masjid (Friday Mosque) is the largest mosque in India, with three huge domes, a pair of minarets over 40 m (131 ft) tall and a courtyard large enough to hold 25,000 worshippers. The mosque took six years to build, employed 5,000 masons and cost around a million rupees, and its soaring minarets and domes remain one of Old Delhi's most memorable sights.*

**Detail in the main prayer hall**

*Grand entrance to the Jama Masjid*

🟢 Visitors to the mosque are required to dress respectfully (no shorts, short skirts or sleeveless tops). It is a good idea to wear appropriate clothing, although shawls are provided.

🟢 There is nowhere to eat or drink within the mosque itself, although the famous Karim's *(see p85)* is close by, and many *dhabas* (roadside cafés) line the surrounding streets.

- Map H4
- Off Netaji Subhash Marg
- Chawri Bazaar Metro
- Open daily 8am until 30 minutes before sunset (at certain times of the day visitors may need to wait for prayers to finish before entering)
- Camera Rs.200 (there are no facilities for leaving your camera at the entrance)

## Top 10 Features

1. The Eastern Approach
2. Meena Bazaar
3. Tomb of Maulana Azad
4. Wrestling and Massage
5. The Courtyard
6. The Façade
7. The Domes
8. The Minarets
9. South Minaret Views
10. Prayer Hall

### ⒈ The Eastern Approach

The most dramatic approach to the magnificent Jama Masjid is from the east, between the busy stalls of the Meena Bazaar, with the mosque looming ahead atop its raised terrace.

### ⒉ Meena Bazaar

This busy market on the eastern approach sells prayer rugs, framed Koranic inscriptions and other Islamic items *(above)*, amidst the fragrant smoke of kebabs from the dozens of nearby *dhabas*.

### ⒊ Tomb of Maulana Azad

Halfway along Meena Bazaar, an opening on the right leads up to a raised tomb *(right)*, which shelters the remains of Maulana Azad (1888–1958), a major figure in the Indian Independence Movement.

### ⒋ Wrestling and Massage

Traditional wrestling matches are held in Urdu Park, near the tomb of Maulana Azad, every Sunday at 4pm. The park is also popular with traditional masseurs, who ply their trade on mats laid on the grass.

*The name Jama Masjid means "Friday Mosque", referring to the communal prayers which are held here weekly on Friday.*

### The Façade
**6** The façade of the prayer hall is the most dramatic of any Indian mosque. Ten cusped arches flank the central *iwan* (main arch), indicating the direction of Mecca and providing a focus of prayer to worshippers in the courtyard.

### The Courtyard
**5** Designed as a place for communal worship, the enormous, breezy courtyard *(above)* has space for thousands of worshippers.

### The Domes
**7** Three huge onion domes *(above)* sit atop the main prayer hall, their bulbous outlines picked out in delicate black stripes. The central dome is partially obscured by the massive *iwan* in front, an architectural conundrum that even Shah Jahan's master architects were unable to resolve.

### The Minarets
**8** The main prayer hall is framed by two minarets *(left)*, their slender outlines adding a counterbalancing lightness to the long façade, topped with Hindu-style *chattris* (pavilions), and visible from all over the old city.

### South Minaret Views
**9** The South Minaret affords unrivalled views of Old Delhi, although the 120 steps are very narrow, and there is not much space at the top.

### Prayer Hall **10**
On the western side of the courtyard is the *liwan* (prayer hall) *(right)*, its western wall punctuated by no less than seven *mihrabs* (niches indicating the direction of Mecca). A *minbar* (pulpit) stands to the right.

## Shah Jahan: Master Builder

Mughal Emperor Shah Jahan was a prolific builder who, during his 30-year reign, oversaw an architectural outpouring that has never been matched. In addition to the Jama Masjid and the Red Fort, he also commissioned extensive additions to the Agra Fort *(see p32)*, and oversaw a spate of works in Lahore, Pakistan (including the Shalimar Gardens and Jahangir's Tomb); not to mention the superb Taj Mahal *(see pp30–31)*.

# ⑩ Humayun's Tomb

*Built in the 1560s, this gigantic mausoleum is the first of the great Mughal garden tombs and the final resting place of the ill-fated emperor Humayun (r.1530–56). The mausoleum is one of Delhi's most impressive sights and a classic example of the great tradition of tomb-building which, almost 100 years later, was to reach its zenith in the Taj Mahal. It is also one of the most peaceful places in Delhi, with a huge expanse of beautiful gardens and an absorbing cluster of further tombs, gateways and mosques to explore.*

Detail inside the Tomb of Isa Khan

🕑 Walking clockwise around the exterior of the tomb before going inside gives a sense of the scale of the mausoleum, and also takes in the Barber's Tomb and Nila Gumbad, after which the tomb can be entered via the southern entrance, three-quarters of the way around.

🍴 There is a pleasant outdoor drinks stall in the Arab Serai.

---

- Map S6
- Off Mathura Road
- Taxi or auto-rickshaw
- Open daily sunrise–sunset
- Rs.250 (Indian citizens Rs.10)
- Video Rs.25

## Top 10 Features

1. Bu Halima's Garden
2. The Arab Serai
3. The Western Gateway
4. The Gardens
5. The Tomb
6. The Barber's Tomb
7. Sabz Burj
8. The Interior
9. Nila Gumbad
10. Mosque and Tomb of Isa Khan

### Bu Halima's Garden
Entrance to the complex is through Bu Halima's garden, complete with its own gateway. This pre-dates the tomb itself, although the mausoleum and garden were designed in alignment to it.

### The Arab Serai
This extensive walled garden is where visiting craftsmen are thought to have lived while they worked on the tomb. It also houses the neat little Afsarwala Mosque and Tomb *(above)*.

### The Western Gateway
Entrance to the gardens is via the western gateway. This serves as a kind of architectural curtain, designed to conceal the garden and tomb from view until the last minute, when Humayun's mausoleum appears in all its glory.

### The Gardens
The beautiful gardens *(left)* that surround the tomb follow the Persian-style *charbagh* pattern, in which the garden is divided into four quarters by water channels: a representation of the Islamic gardens of paradise.

*The western walls inside Mughal tombs are typically decorated with a* mihrab, *indicating the direction of Mecca.*

### 5 The Tomb
The tomb *(left)* itself stands on a large raised platform; each of its four façades is dominated by a huge arch, topped by a massive dome.

### 6 The Barber's Tomb
According to legend, this elegant tomb was built for the imperial barber – a fitting memorial to the person trusted to hold a razor to the emperor's throat.

### 7 Sabz Burj
Housing the grave of an unknown Mughal nobleman, this beautiful blue-domed, Persian-style tomb *(below)* now stands dramatically marooned at a busy roundabout near the entrance to the complex.

### 8 The Interior
A single door on the southern side opens into the interior of the tomb, where Humayun lies in solitary splendour in a small and ostentatiously plain marble tomb.

### 9 Nila Gumbad
Located just outside the gardens, the striking Persian-style Nila Gumbad, with its blue-tiled dome, houses the remains of an unknown Mughal nobleman.

### 10 Mosque and Tomb of Isa Khan
The florid octagonal mosque and tomb of Isa Khan *(below)*, a courtier during the reign of Sher Shah Suri (r.1540–45), provides a complete change of style. Both mosque and tomb lie within their own garden, enclosed in fortress-like walls.

#### Humayun
The second Mughal emperor, Humayun, was an endearingly irresolute figure who alternated between bouts of military brilliance and self-indulgence. He succeeded his father Babur in 1530, but promptly lost his empire to the Afghan invader Sher Shah Suri, and had to seek refuge in Persia for the next 15 years before winning it back. One year later he was dead, after falling down a steep flight of steps in the Purana Qila (see p89).

# 🔟 Around Rajpath

*Running east to west through the heart of New Delhi, Rajpath (formerly Kingsway) is the grandest of all the city's boulevards, stretching some 2 km (1 mile) from India Gate to the presidential palace, Rashtrapati Bhavan. Rajpath was created to showcase spectacular processions and occasions of state, while the surrounding government buildings were intended to serve as an enduring symbol of British pomp and power to rival – or, indeed, surpass – those monuments left scattered around the city by previous rulers.*

*Coat-of-arms on the Secretariat Building*

⚙ All the major government buildings on Rajpath, including Sansad Bhavan and the Secretariat are closed to the public. The three roads encircling Sansad Bhavan are also closed, so the Cathedral Church of the Redemption can only be accessed from the north.

🍴 There are very few places to eat and drink along Rajpath, although the grassy verges that flank Rajpath make an excellent spot for a picnic. The National Museum nearby houses a pleasant café to relax in.

• Map L3
• Central Secretariat Metro
• Rashtrapati Bhavan tours: Call in advance on 2301 5321

## Top 10 Features

1 India Gate
2 Rajpath
3 Sansad Bhavan
4 Cathedral Church of the Redemption
5 Raisina Hill
6 Vijay Chowk
7 Secretariat Buildings
8 Military Parades
9 Rashtrapati Bhavan
🔟 Mughal Gardens

### 1 India Gate

This imposing arch *(above)* commemorates the 90,000 Indian soldiers killed in World War I and the Afghan Wars. Below the arch, the Tomb of the Unknown Soldier honours the dead of the Indo-Pakistan conflict of 1971.

### 2 Rajpath

This grand 2-km (1-mile) axis connects India Gate with Rashtrapati Bhavan linking many of New Delhi's major buildings along the way.

### 3 Sansad Bhavan

The huge Sansad Bhavan (1935), a distinctive circular building north of Rajpath, was built for the Legislative Assembly and is now home to the Indian parliament. An impressive structure, it is set at a distance from Rajpath, reflecting Britain's grudging attitude towards Indian democratic aspirations.

### 4 Cathedral Church of the Redemption

Designed by Henry Medd, assistant to British architect Herbert Baker (1862–1946), this Neo-Classical church (1935) *(left)* was inspired by Palladio's Il Redentore in Venice, and is one of the largest and most impressive in Delhi.

*For further information on Rajpath's military parades see p40.*

### 5 Raisina Hill

Raisina Hill *(above)* climbs between the Secretariat Buildings towards Rashtrapati Bhavan, although the latter only becomes visible once you get to the top, a miscalculation that infuriated Lutyens.

### 6 Vijay Chowk

Formerly known as the Grand Place, this huge crossroads marks the point at which Rajpath meets Raisina Hill.

### 7 Secretariat Buildings

Flanking Raisina Hill are the Secretariat Buildings *(above)*. Designed by Herbert Baker in Neo-Classical style with Indian touches, they now house government offices.

### 8 Military Parades

The Republic Day parade (26 Jan) features a show of military personnel and colourful floats from every Indian state. Beating the Retreat (29 Jan), held on Raisina Hill, is a performance of military bands.

### 9 Rashtrapati Bhavan

Once the viceroy's residence and now home to the Indian President, the magnificent Rashtrapati Bhavan *(below)* is Lutyens' masterpiece, a uniquely successful fusion of European and Indian elements. Visitors can call in advance for a guided tour on specific days.

### 10 Mughal Gardens

Within the grounds of Rashtrapati Bhavan, this beautiful oasis *(above)* is laid out with water-courses, fountains and neat squares of lawn.

> **Edwin Lutyens**
>
> Edwin Landseer Lutyens (1869–1944), the master architect behind New Delhi, worked for over 20 years on the new city. He developed a unique Indian-influenced Neo-Classical style, best seen in the grand Rashtrapati Bhavan with its huge Buddhist-inspired dome. The success of Lutyens' designs is all the more surprising given his self-confessed dislike of Indian architecture.

# Qutb Minar Complex

*Towering over southern Delhi, the monumental Qutb Minar is one of the city's most dramatic and instantly recognizable landmarks: a triumphal minaret that marked with a flourish both the coming of Islam to the subcontinent and the arrival of the Delhi sultans (see p43). Further remarkable monuments, including India's oldest mosque, lie scattered at the foot of the minaret and nearby, around Mehrauli Village.*

Detail of a pillar in Quwwat-ul-Islam

Ceiling at the entrance of the Quwwat-ul-Islam

🔵 The Qutb Minar is one of Delhi's busiest tourist attractions. Arrive early or late in the day to avoid the coach parties.

🔵 There are plenty of drink stalls around the entrance to the Qutb complex, but none inside it. For food, it is best to bring a picnic.

• Map U3
• Mehrauli, Delhi-Gurgaon Road
• Taxi, auto-rickshaw or Qutb Minar Metro
• Open daily sunrise–sunset
• Rs.250 (Indian citizens Rs.10)
• Video Rs.25, audio guide Rs.100

## Top 10 Features

1. Quwwat-ul-Islam
2. The Central Courtyard
3. Madrasa of Alauddin Khilji
4. Tomb of Imam Zamin
5. Iron Pillar
6. Qutb Minar
7. Alai Minar
8. Tomb of Iltutmish
9. Alai Darwaza
10. The Prayer Hall Screen

### Quwwat-ul-Islam

The first mosque in India, the Quwwat-ul-Islam *(below)* (Might of Islam) was built by Qutbuddin Aibak (r.1206–10) in 1192, soon after Muhammad Ghori's conquest of northwest India *(see p36)*.

### The Central Courtyard

Aibak demolished 27 Hindu and Jain temples to make way for his mosque. The temple pillars were incorporated into the arcade of the central courtyard *(below)*, giving it a Hindu appearance.

### Madrasa of Alauddin Khilji

Built around 1317 as a *madrasa* (religious school), this large, plain building has now lost most of its original stone facing. Alauddin (r.1296–1316) himself is thought to be buried in the central chamber of this structure.

*The so-called Delhi sultans held power across much of northern India for over 400 years, until the coming of the Mughals.*

**Tomb of Imam Zamin**
This tomb *(above)* houses the remains of the Turkestani religious itinerant Imam Zamin (d.1539) and postdates the rest of the complex.

**Iron Pillar**
This unusual pillar, in the central courtyard, is thought to have been made in Bihar in the 4th century and later brought to Delhi by the Tomars. Remarkably, it has remained rust free for over 1,500 years.

**Qutb Minar**
Built during the reigns of Aibak and Iltutmish (r.1211–36), this minaret *(left)* is 72 m (236 ft) tall. A fifth storey, clad in marble, was added later after the summit was damaged by lightning.

**Alai Minar**
A stump of rough stone *(above)* is all that remains of a maverick scheme to construct a second over-sized minaret, intended to surpass even the mighty Qutb Minar.

**Tomb of Iltutmish**
Immediately behind the mosque is the tomb of Iltutmish *(left)*, one of the principal architects of the Qutb complex. Small and plain on the outside, the tomb is lavishly carved within.

**Alai Darwaza**
Built in 1311 as a new gateway *(below)* to the mosque, the Alai Darwaza is richly carved using red sandstone and white marble, a hallmark of the later Mughal style.

**The Tower of Babel, Delhi Style**

Probably the grandest folly in the history of Delhi, the Alai Minar was the brainchild of Alauddin Khilji, the most brilliant and ruthless of all the Delhi sultans. The plan was to build a minaret twice the height of the Qutb Minar, but the gargantuan project never really got off the ground, and all that remains is a large stump of rubble – "a frustrated tower of Babel", as one writer neatly describes it.

**The Prayer Hall Screen**
One of the finest pieces of Islamic architecture in India, the Quwwat-ul-Islam's prayer hall screen is composed of five narrow, sharply pointed arches, covered in a profusion of Koranic inscriptions and bands of beautiful floral decoration.

Left **Façade of the Madhi Masjid** Right **Adham Khan's tomb**

# Sites Around Mehrauli

### 1 Mehrauli Archaeological Park

Stretching west of the Qutb Minar complex, the Mehrauli Archaeological Park was established to protect the many ancient monuments scattered around the area, including over 100 in the park itself, dating from the 11th to the 19th centuries.

### 2 Jamali-Kamali Masjid and Tomb

This beautiful early Mughal mosque, built by the poet Sheikh Fazlullah (known as Jamali; d.1535), has a delicately carved façade and characteristic red sandstone and white marble stonework. The poet's pretty little tomb is located in a tranquil enclosure beside the mosque.

**Exquisite interior of the Jamali-Kamali Tomb**

### 3 Adham Khan's Tomb

Mughal Emperor Akbar built this tomb for his foster brother, who was thrown to his death from the battlements of the Agra Fort for murdering Akbar's prime minister. Its labyrinthine interior has earned it the nickname of *bhulbhulaiyan* (maze).

**Detail of Quli Khan's tomb**

### 4 Quli Khan's Tomb

Erected for Adham Khan's brother, Mohammad Quli Khan, this neat little tomb was converted by Sir Thomas Metcalfe into a summer retreat, christened Dilkusha, whose ruined walls can still be seen surrounding the tomb.

### 5 Balban's Tomb

Close to the Jamali-Kamali Masjid lie the fragments of the tomb of Balban (1200–87), one of the most powerful of the early Delhi sultans.

### 6 Madhi Masjid

Built in the early Mughal era, this heavily fortified building looks more like a fortress than a mosque, with a large courtyard and – unusually – two separate prayer halls on either side of a central *mihrab* wall.

### 7 Dargah Qutb Sahib

In the heart of the Mehrauli bazaar (ask locally for directions), this serene little religious complex commemorates Qutbuddin Bakhtiyar Kaki (d.1235), a Sufi

For a detailed account of all the monuments around Mehrauli, see Lucy Peck's Delhi: A Thousand Years of Building **see p106**.

saint from Fergana (in modern Uzbekistan). The complex contains a cluster of religious buildings as well as the saint's grave, enclosed by a delicate latticed screen.

### Rajon ki Bain

Built in 1506, this superb *boali* (step-well) is atmospherically buried amidst woodland in the heart of the park. It is built over four levels, with rooms and arcades around the top two floors and a well below.

**Arcaded levels of Rajon ki Bain**

### Zafar Mahal

Located close to the Dargah Qutb Sahib, this summer palace was built by Emperor Akbar Shah II (1760–1837) and contains various structures, including the tombs of two Mughal emperors and the pretty little Moti Masjid.

### Jahaz Mahal

At the far western end of Mehrauli Village, this enigmatic Lodi-era structure is thought to have been either a travellers' rest house or a royal pleasure palace.

# Metcalfe's Folly

*Mehrauli witnessed one of the stranger episodes in Anglo-Indian cultural history when Sir Thomas Theophilus Metcalfe (1795–1853), British Resident at the Mughal Court, decided to establish a summer residence in the area. Rather than build a new house, Metcalfe made the unusual decision to convert the historic Mughal tomb of Quli Khan into an English-style country residence, which he christened Dilkusha (Heart's Delight),*

**The quiet tomb of Quli Khan amidst verdant surroundings**

*although it is generally known as Metcalfe's Folly. The tomb's central chamber was turned into a dining room; a pair of flanking wings and various outbuildings were erected (remnants of which can still be seen) and a string of Indian-style follies were built in the surrounding countryside, including a prominent chattri (open-sided pavilion) on a nearby hill. As fate would have it, Metcalfe's love of all things Mughal did him little good: he died allegedly poisoned by one of the emperor's queens.*

# Crafts Museum

*Delhi's most enjoyable museum showcases India's incredible variety of local artistic and cultural traditions in a rustic building and walled garden designed by Charles Correa (b.1930). There are crafts here from every part of the subcontinent and in every type of medium, from tribal costumes to ivory carvings, including a complete miniature village of traditional buildings from across India in the grounds outside.*

Gem-studded necklace

Kohbarghar *by Ganga Devi, 1990*

⏩ The museum is a good place to shop for crafts, but as ever it pays to do some research beforehand. First visit the government emporiums around Connaught Place to find out what is available and to get an idea of prices.

☕ There is a small café just inside the museum entrance serving drinks and simple meals.

- Map R3
- Bhairon Marg
- 233 71370
- Pragati Maidan Metro
- Open Tue–Sun 10am–5pm
- Rs.150 (Indian citizens Rs.10)
- *Permission for photography can be obtained from the reception*

## Top 10 Features

1. The Museum Building
2. Resident Craftspeople
3. Bhuta Sculpture Gallery
4. Folk and Tribal Art
5. Cultic Objects Gallery
6. Courtly Crafts Gallery
7. Traditional Buildings
8. Outdoor Exhibits
9. Textile Gallery
10. Shopping for Crafts

### 1 The Museum Building

Designed by Indian architect Charles Correa, this rustic ochre building, encircled by shady verandahs and set within a tree-filled compound, feels like a rural village in the heart of urban Delhi.

### 2 Resident Craftspeople

At the back of the museum is a courtyard, home to a selection of stalls where artisans can often be seen at work on a wide range of crafts, including painting, stone carving, metalworking and weaving.

### 3 Bhuta Sculpture Gallery

Devoted to the Bhuta cult of Karnataka, this gallery *(left)* contains striking images from the shrine of Nandikeshvara in Udipi province, carved in dark jackfruit wood and featuring human and animal-headed figures.

### 4 Folk and Tribal Art

This gallery is packed with unusual objects dating from the 19th century to the present day, from a collection of traditional dolls *(left)* to religious items and devotional images.

### 5 Cultic Objects Gallery

A collection of religious objects *(left)* from across India, ranging from Hindu bronzes and South Indian paintings to Jain and Tibetan Buddhist artifacts including a carved Jain shrine from Gujarat.

### 6 Courtly Crafts Gallery

A display of aristocratic arts from the 18th century to today, including exquisitely detailed *bidri*-ware (silver inlay work), enamelware, jade, glass jewellery and outstanding ivory carvings.

### 7 Traditional Buildings

Scattered around the museum garden is a fascinating collection of traditional buildings from across India, including a men's house from Nagaland *(above)* supported by Amerindian-looking totem poles.

### Key to Floorplan

- Ground Floor
- First Floor

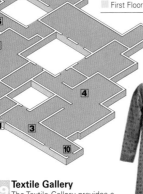

### 8 Outdoor Exhibits

A number of exhibits are dotted around the museum grounds such as stone carvings from Rajasthan *(above)* and a striking group of Chinese-looking statues from Tamil Nadu depicting Aiyanna – a village guardian, said to ride on a ghostly horse, chasing away evil spirits.

### 9 Textile Gallery

The Textile Gallery provides a comprehensive overview of India's myriad textile traditions, with a vast collection of fabrics in every kind of style, including brocade, block printing, tie-dye and appliqué.

### 10 Shopping for Crafts

The museum has one of Delhi's most interesting selections of traditional crafts for sale, either from one of the artisans or outdoor stalls at the back of the museum, or from the shop at the entrance.

### Gallery Guide

The Crafts Museum is relatively small and can be covered in a couple of hours. All the galleries are laid out over the ground floor of the building, except the Textile Gallery and a section of the Courtly Crafts Gallery, which are tucked away upstairs and easy to miss.

# Top 10 Lodi Gardens

*One of the most enjoyable excursions in Delhi, the beautiful Lodi Gardens offer a winning combination of nature and history. The gardens themselves are among the most attractive and relaxed in the city, with quiet paths winding between tropical trees and plentiful birdlife in the branches overhead. Historical interest is provided by the series of fine medieval tombs dotted among the trees and lawns, erected by nobles of the Lodi and Sayyid dynasties during the later years of the Delhi Sultanate.*

*Bara Gumbad Masjid*

🔁 The Lodi Gardens are easily combined with a visit to nearby Safdarjung's Tomb (see p90).

🍴 There is nowhere to eat or drink in the gardens, although the India Habitat Centre, close to the southern entrance to the gardens on Lodi Road, has a couple of attractive cafés.

- Map N6
- Lodi Road
- Taxi, auto-rickshaw or Race Course Metro
- Open Apr–Sep daily 5am–8pm; Oct–Mar daily 6am–8pm

## Top 10 Features

1. The Gardens
2. Sikander Lodi's Tomb
3. National Bonsai Garden
4. Bara Gumbad Tomb
5. Bara Gumbad Masjid
6. Round Tower
7. Muhammad Shah's Tomb
8. Shish Gumbad
9. Birdlife
10. Athpula

### The Gardens
The gardens *(above)* were created in 1936 by Lady Willingdon, wife of the viceroy, who had the two villages that formerly stood here demolished to make way for the new gardens.

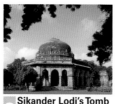

### Sikander Lodi's Tomb
At the northern end of the gardens is the tomb *(above)* of Sikander Lodi (r.1489–1517), the penultimate Delhi sultan. Occupying an idyllic garden, its interior walls are have the remains of beautiful blue tilework.

### National Bonsai Garden
Near the southern entrance to the park, the National Bonsai Garden sports a small collection of tiny trees, and some interesting displays on the various styles of traditional bonsai.

### Bara Gumbad Tomb
Dating from around 1500, the Bara Gumbad Tomb is the gardens' most impressive structure, a large and imposing cuboid tomb (occupant unknown), topped by a massive dome. Its rather severe outlines are relieved by alternating panels of red and black stone, which are used to pick out the details around the doors and windows.

For more on the Delhi sultans and their architecture see pp42–3.

### Bara Gumbad Masjid
Attached to the Bara Gumbad Tomb, this mosque *(above)* is small but lavishly decorated, with swirls of Koranic script covering every available surface.

### Round Tower
East of the Bara Gumbad stands a solid-looking round tower, probably dating from the 14th century.

### Muhammad Shah's Tomb
The tomb of Sayyid ruler Muhammad Shah (r.1434–44) is built in the octagonal shape favoured by the later Delhi sultans, its main dome surrounded by eight small *chattris*.

### Shish Gumbad
Built around 1600 for an unidentified nobleman, this is a cuboid-shaped tomb *(above)* enlivened with bands of rich blue tiles which run around the middle and top.

### Birdlife
The gardens are home to a rich array of birdlife *(left)*, including colourful tree pies and blue throats as well as diminutive spotted owlets, geese and raucous flocks of bright green parakeets.

### Athpula
Located near the tomb of Sikander Lodi, the striking Athpula (Eight Piers) bridge *(below)* was built during the reign of Akbar (r.1556–1605).

### The Sayyid and Lodi Dynasties
The Sayyid and Lodi dynasties held sway from 1414 until 1526, although their power was challenged by a series of internal rebellions and external threats. The first Sayyid sultan, Khizr Khan, rose to power after Timur's invasion in 1398; while the last sultan, Ibrahim Lodi (r.1517–26), was killed by Timur's great-great-great-grandson, Babur – founder of the Mughal Dynasty.

# 🔟 National Museum

*Founded in 1949, the superb National Museum is India's finest, with a collection of over 200,000 exhibits charting five millennia of subcontinental history. Every major strand in India's complex cultural identity is covered here, with artifacts from across the country and beyond, including prehistoric archaeological finds, Buddhist statues, Chola bronzes and Mughal miniatures, as well as many Central Asian artworks.*

Bronze statue of Kali

Sculpture outside the National Museum

🔄 The collection is huge, so don't try to see everything at once. A useful audioguide (Rs.150) picks out around 30 of the best exhibits.

🔄 There is an attractive café on the top floor.

- Map N3
- Janpath
- 2301 8415
- Central Secretariat Metro
- Rs.300 (Indian citizens Rs.10)
- Camera Rs.300 (Rs.20)
- www. nationalmuseumindia. gov.in
- The first and second floors are currently under renovation. Please call ahead to check.

## Top 10 Features

1. Dancing Girl
2. Kali
3. Asita's Visit to Suddhadhana
4. Ganga
5. Mughal Emperor Shah Jahan in Dara Shikoh's Marriage Procession
6. Shiva Nataraja
7. Avalokitesvara
8. Neminatha
9. Gandharan Buddha
10. Baluchari Sari

### 1 Dancing Girl

Small but famous image of an elegant, long-legged dancing girl *(right)*, found in Mohenjodaro and dating from around 2500 BC – one of the world's oldest cast-bronze statuettes.

### 2 Kali
A superb late 12th-century bronze in which the fearsome goddess Kali, one of the Cholas' favoured deities, appears serenely poised and unusually benign.

### 3 Asita's Visit to Suddhadhana

Beautifully carved panel *(right)* from the great Satavahana-era Buddhist monastery of Amaravati (in Andhra Pradesh), dating from the 1st–2nd century AD and showing the sage Asita visiting King Suddhadhana to admire his son, the newly born Buddha.

*The museum's exhibits were first displayed in 1949 in Rashtrapati Bhavan, until the new museum building opened in 1960.*

### 4 Ganga
This 5th-century Gupta terracotta statue *(left)* is one of the museum's most graceful images. The river goddess Ganga, accompanied by an attendant, is seen walking on the back of her mythical animal mount, the crocodile-like *makara* (mythical creature), whilst carrying an urn containing water from the sacred river.

### 6 Shiva Nataraja
One of the museum's most famous exhibits, this iconic 12th-century Chola bronze *(above)* shows a four-armed Shiva performing the *nataraj*, or cosmic dance, surrounded by a ring of fire.

### 5 Mughal Emperor Shah Jahan in Dara Shikoh's Marriage Procession
Painted around 1750 in Awadh, this painting is a good example of superbly detailed Indian miniature art *(centre)*, portraying the wedding procession of Shah Jahan's favourite son and preferred heir, Dara Shikoh.

### 7 Avalokitesvara
This rare pair of 9th- and 10th-century silk paintings *(left)*, from the town of Dunhuang on the old Silk Route in north-western China, shows Avalokitesvara, the Boddhisatva (the Buddha) of Infinite Compassion – just two of the many exhibits amassed by the British-Hungarian archaeologist Aurel Stein.

### Gallery Guide
The collection is arranged over three floors, though almost all the best exhibits are on the ground floor. Exhibits 1 to 9 are on the ground floor while exhibit 10 is on the first floor. The museum holds a film show on Art and Culture *(Tue–Sun at 11:30am, 2:30pm and 4pm)* that is a must-see. There is also a shop near the reception where there are replicas of some of the exhibits and books for sale. A visit to the extensive library can be valuable for researchers.

### 8 Neminatha
A simple 11th-century Chahaman image of the 22nd Jain *tirthankara* (guru), Neminatha, who is said to be a contemporary of the great Hindu god Krishna.

### 9 Gandharan Buddha
A beautiful serene standing Buddha, dating from the 2nd century AD, showing the marriage of Greek and Indian influences typical of the art of Gandhara.

### 10 Baluchari Sari
A rare 18th-century silk sari *(below)* with delicate floral patterns from Murshidabad (West Bengal), one of India's most famous centres of silk production.

Left **Gallery of Maurya and Sunga Art** Centre **Sculpture, Medieval Art** Right **Gallery of Gupta Art**

# 10 National Museum Collections

### 1 Harappan Civilization
One of the world's finest showcases of the Harappan (or Indus Valley) Civilization (circa 2500–1500 BC). There is a wide range of finds from Harappa, Mohenjodaro and elsewhere, bringing one of the world's most ancient cultures to vivid life.

### 2 Maurya, Sunga and Satavahana Art
Devoted to the art of the Mauryans (321–185 BC), India's first great empire, and their successors, with monumental sculptures, bas-relief carvings and stone pillars, most recovered from Buddhist temples, including panels from the monastery at Amaravati (see p26).

### 3 Kushan (Gandhara, Mathura and Ikshavaku Art)
This superb collection of classical sculpture from Gandhara (in Afghanistan), famous for its remarkable Indo-Graeco culture, in which local Buddhist traditions intermingled with Greek styles brought to the region by Alexander the Great (356–23 BC).

### 4 Gupta Terracotta and Early Medieval Art
This gallery showcases the classic art of the Guptas (3rd–5th centuries), the second of India's great dynasties, along with more flamboyant statues from the early Pallava (571–668 BC) and Chola (300–1279 BC) kingdoms of the South, with intricately carved Hindu gods.

### 5 Late Medieval Art
An excellent collection of Indian sculpture, with outstanding examples of the sculptural arts that flourished across central and southern India in the Vijayanagar, Hoysala, Chola and Pala kingdoms during the 11th and 12th centuries.

The Bronzes Gallery

### 6 Bronzes
One of the museum's undoubted highlights: a room full of stunning Chola bronze statues of assorted Hindu deities, including one of the most iconic images of Indian art – a pair of Natarajas (Dancing Shivas).

### 7 Buddhist Art
A wide range of Buddhist art and artifacts from across India, Nepal, Gandhara and China,

# Indian Miniature Painting

*Although originally of Persian origin, the art of the miniature was perfected in India, where artists developed a distinctive style of brilliantly coloured and minutely detailed painting, usually depicting either religious subjects or scenes from courtly life. Miniature painting flourished under Muslim patronage throughout India – the Mughals, in particular, commissioned thousands of pictures and illustrated manuscripts, while distinctive regional schools subsequently developed in Rajasthan, the Deccan and across the Pahari region in the Himalayan foothills. Most artists remain anonymous, although a few of the most famous are listed on the left.*

**Kangra painting, circa AD 1800**

1. Mir Sayyid Ali (Persian/Mughal, 16th century)
2. Abd al-Samad (Persian/Mughal, 16th century)
3. Basawan (Mughal, 16th century)
4. Mansur (Mughal, 17th century)
5. Bishandas (Mughal, 17th century)
6. Abu al-Hasan (Mughal, 17th century)
7. Govardhan (Mughal, 17th century)
8. Bichitr (Mughal, 17th century)
9. Sahibdin (Rajasthan, 17th century)
10. Dalchand (Rajasthan, 18th century)

**A colourful Mughal miniature painting**

including rare *tankhas* (devotional paintings), statues, reliquaries and a pair of fine silver-and-brass temple trumpets from Ladakh.

**8 Indian Miniature Paintings**
Another of the museum's highlights, featuring a large collection of superbly detailed and vibrant paintings from the Rajasthani, Pahari, Deccani and Mughal schools.

**9 Decorative Arts and Textiles**
Dedicated to India's rich and varied clothing and textile traditions, this gallery features a colourful display of woven, printed, tie-dyed, embroidered and appliqué-worked fabrics in silk, cotton and wool. Examples of India's varied decorative arts fills the adjoining galleries.

**10 Tribal Lifestyle**
This is a rare glimpse into the lives of India's little-known, Chinese-descended northeastern tribes. Exhibits include simple weapons, household items and some outlandish headgear, backed up by fascinating black-and-white photos of various tribes in traditional attire.

# 🔟 Taj Mahal, Agra

*India's most iconic building, the Taj Mahal was built by Shah Jahan (see p8) for his favourite wife, Arjumand Banu Begum – popularly known as Mumtaz – or "Taj" – Mahal, who married Shah Jahan in 1612 and bore him 14 children before her death in 1631. The emperor's grief found an outlet in the world's most magnificent tomb, a masterpiece in white marble, which took some 20,000 workmen over two decades to build.*

Detail from the Taj Mahal

Detail from the walls on the Taj Mahal

🕐 Arrive very early in the morning to avoid the huge crowds and entrance queues. Stringent security is in force and visitors are not allowed to bring in food, drink, mobile phones or even guidebooks.

🍴 Food and drinks are prohibited inside the Taj (apart from a single bottle of water). There are many backpacker cafés outside in Taj Ganj (try Joney's Place, one of the best) but note that tickets for the Taj are only valid for one entry, so you can't exit for refreshments and then go back in.

• Map C3
• Agra is 215 km (134 miles) south from Delhi.
• Taj Ganj
• Open Sat–Thu 6am–7pm; closed Fri
• Rs.750 (Indian citizens Rs.20)

## Top 10 Features

1 Chowk-i-Jilo Khana
2 The Charbagh
3 The Lotus Pool
4 Mosque and Mehman Khana
5 Pietra Dura
6 Calligraphic Panels
7 The Tomb
8 The Dome
9 Minarets
10 Tomb Chamber

### 1 Chowk-i-Jilo Khana

The Chowk-i-Jilo Khana is a forecourt *(below)*, from where a gateway leads into the garden, serving as a screen to the Taj Mahal itself.

### 2 The Charbagh

The Taj sits at the far end of one of the finest Mughal *charbagh*-style gardens *(below)*, an idyllic expanse of lawn divided into four by raised marble water channels.

### 3 The Lotus Pool

The centre of the *charbagh's* four inter-secting water channels is marked by the beautiful white marble Lotus Pool, symbolizing *al-Hawd al-Kawthar*, the celestial pool in the Islamic gardens of paradise.

### 4 Mosque and Mehman Khana

The Taj is flanked by two mirror-image build-ings: on one side a large mosque; on the other, the Mehman Khana, or *jawab* (res-ponse). The mosque is still in use, but the *jawab* cannot be used for worship since it is oriented the wrong way round.

*Mumtaz Mahal was engaged to Shah Jahan when she was just 14 years old, although they didn't get married until five years later.*

### Pietra Dura
**5** Large parts of the Taj Mahal's exterior walls are covered in excellent pietra dura *(left)* inlay work, in which intricate stylized geometrical floral patterns are created using a variety of coloured precious and semi-precious gemstones.

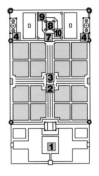

### Calligraphic Panels
**6** Koranic inscriptions *(below)* frame the tomb's four archways, picked out in black marble. The script in the higher panels is enlarged to compensate for the distorting effects of perspective.

### The Tomb
**7** The classic perfection of the Taj is rooted in the simplest of architectural concepts. The main tomb is a perfect cube, while the dome itself is of equal height to the building on which it rests.

### The Dome
**8** The onion dome rises to a height of 73 m (239 ft), topped by a lotus-shaped design and surrounded by four smaller *chattris* (domed pavilions), echoing those that cap the four minarets.

### Minarets
**9** Four minarets mark each corner. Unusually, these are detached from the main tomb, so that if any of them ever fell, they would collapse away from the main tomb, causing less damage.

### Tomb Chamber
**10** The tomb of Mumtaz Mahal *(below)* sits at the centre of the atmospheric, tomb chamber, protected by an exquisitely detailed *jali* (carved screen), while that of Shah Jahan lies alongside it.

### The Black Taj
Of the many strange myths that have grown up around the Taj, the most frequently repeated is that Shah Jahan intended to build a second mausoleum for himself, built entirely of black marble, and facing the original Taj across the Yamuna River. The idea was first mooted by Frenchman Jean-Baptiste Tavernier (1605–89), who visited Agra in 1665. There is, however, no evidence to support this appealing but fanciful theory.

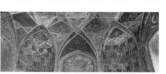

Left **Sandstone tomb of Mariam Zamani** Right **Colourful ceiling of Chini-ka-Rauza**

# 🔟 Sights in Agra

### Mehtab Bagh
The Mehtab Bagh (Moonlight Garden) offers the ultimate view of the Taj Mahal, framed between its minarets in picture-perfect splendour on the far side of the the Yamuna River – particularly magical, as the name suggests, when the moon is full. According to legend, this is also the spot where Shah Jahan intended to build his Black Taj *(see p31)* although nothing has been found to support this theory. 🔊 *Map C3 • Open daily sunrise–sunset • Adm*

### Taj Nature Walk
Just east of the Taj Mahal, the Taj Nature Walk is an attractive area of wooded parkland – a sylvan retreat from the crowded city, with fine views of the Taj itself. 🔊 *Map C3 • Open daily 9am–6:30pm • Adm*

### Itimad-ud-Daulah
Built by Nur Jahan (1577–1645), the all-powerful wife of Jahangir, for her father, Mirza Ghiyas Beg, this tomb is modest in size but exquisitely decorated, prefiguring the Taj Mahal in the

**Floral patterns at Itimad-ud-Daulah**

profusion of pietra dura inlay work which covers every part of the exterior. 🔊 *Map C3 • Open daily sunrise–sunset • Adm*

### Agra Fort
The magnificent Agra Fort was originally built by Akbar (1542–1605) and successively enlarged and embellished by Jahangir (1569–1627) and Shah Jahan, with a fascinating array of palaces, pavilions and mosques in a wide variety of styles – from Jahangir's solid Hindu-influenced Jahangiri Mahal to Shah Jahan's delicate white marble constructions. 🔊 *Map C3 • Open daily sunrise–sunset • Adm and charge for video*

### Jama Masjid
Built in 1648, this spectacular mosque is a perfect example of the late-Mughal architectural style perfected during the reign of Shah Jahan. The building is reminiscent of the great Jama Masjid in Delhi *(see pp12–13)*: fronted by a large courtyard, with a red sandstone prayer hall topped by a trio of shapely domes atop. 🔊 *Map C3 • Open daily sunrise–sunset*

### Kinari Bazaar
Spread around the foot of the Jama Masjid, this is the most atmospheric of Agra's various bazaars, home to the city's celebrated purveyors of *petha*, an unusual confection made from crystallized pumpkin. 🔊 *Map C3 • Open Mon–Sat 11:30am–6pm*

## Top 10 Mughal Dates

1. 1504: Sikandar Lodi moves his capital from Delhi to Agra.
2. 1526: Humayun captures Agra after the defeat of the Lodi sultans at Panipat.
3. 1530: Babur dies and is buried at Agra in the Rambagh Gardens.
4. 1565: Construction of Agra Fort begins.
5. 1571: Mughal court moves to the new city of Fatehpur Sikri.
6. 1612: Completion of Sikandra by Jahangir.
7. 1628: Completion of Itimad-ud-Daulah.
8. 1638: Shah Jahan moves capital to new city of Shahjahanabad.
9. 1653: Completion of the Taj Mahal.
10. 1658: Shah Jahan is imprisoned at the Taj by his son, Aurangzeb.

# Imperial City of the Mughals

*For most of the Mughal era, it was Agra that was the most important city of the empire. Although Humayun had begun work on a new citadel in Delhi – the Purana Qila (see p89) – his far more capable son, Akbar, had little interest in the old capital and spent most of his time in Agra instead (or in his new city of Fatehpur Sikri). It was under Akbar that Agra rose to pre-eminence. Only late in Shah Jahan's reign did Delhi begin to rival Agra's Imperial splendour. Even then, he chose Agra as the site of the Taj Mahal.*

Spectacular red sandstone façade of the Agra Fort

### Chini-ka-Rauza

7 This distinctive, if rather dilapidated, Persian-style tomb was built between 1628 and 1639 for Afzal Khan, a poet from Shiraz, who served as a minister under Shah Jahan. The tomb is covered in delicately coloured tiles. ◈ *Map C3 • Open daily*

### Rambagh Gardens

8 These extensive formal gardens – laid out in the traditional Persian *charbagh* plan – are where Babur (1483–1530), founder of the Mughal Dynasty, was originally buried, although his remains were later exhumed and taken to Kabul. ◈ *Map C3 • Open daily sunrise–sunset • Adm*

### Sikandra

9 The last resting place of Akbar, the huge mausoleum of Sikandra is one of the grandest of all Mughal monuments, although something of an architectural hotch-potch, with the usual rooftop dome replaced with a strange four-storey pavilion. ◈ *Map C3 • Open daily sunrise–sunset • Adm*

### Mariam's Tomb

10 Decaying but atmospheric, this sandstone tomb was erected in honour of Mariam Zamani, one of the most important of Akbar's 300 or so wives and mother of Jahangir. ◈ *Map C3 • Open daily sunrise–sunset • Adm*

Left **Tughlaq gold coin** Centre **Qutb Minar** Right **A painting of the 1857 Uprising**

# Moments in History

**AD 736: Founding of Delhi**
Delhi was founded by the Rajput Tomars in the Surajkund area, south of the modern city. In 1060, the town was relocated 10 km (6 miles) north by Tomar ruler Anangpal II, who created a new fortified citadel there called Lal Kot. Around 1160 the Tomars became vassals of the Chauhans, another Rajput clan from Ajmer, who extended Lal Kot and renamed it Qila Rai Pithora.

**1192: Founding of the Delhi Sultanate**
Muhammad of Ghori, from Ghazni (in Afghanistan), invaded north India in 1191 but was defeated by Prithviraj Chauhan III at the Battle of Tarain. A year later, Muhammad returned, defeated Prithviraj and took control of northern India. He then returned home, leaving Qutbuddin Aibak, his general, in charge of Delhi. Aibak became the first sultan of Delhi following Muhammad Ghori's death in 1206.

**1327: To Daulatabad and Back Again**
The ruler Muhammad bin Tughlaq moved the capital from Delhi to Daulatabad (present-day Devagiri), 1,500 km (932 miles) to the south. Delhi's entire population was forcibly relocated to the new city. Daulatabad, however,

lasted only two years before Tughlaq abandoned it and returned to Delhi.

**1398: Invasion of Timur**
A Mongol army led by Timur the Lame, or Tamerlaine as he is known in the West, sacked Delhi and left it in ruins, leading to the fall of the Tughlaq Dynasty.

**1526: Arrival of the First Mughals**
Babur, a Central Asian adventurer and former ruler of Fergana, Kabul and Samarkand, defeated the last Delhi sultan, Ibrahim Lodi, at the Battle of Panipat (1526) and ushered in the Mughal Dynasty.

**1638: Foundation of Shajahanabad**
The fifth Mughal emperor, Shah Jahan, moved the capital from Agra (where it had been moved by his predecessor, Akbar) back to Delhi and founded the city of Shahjahanabad, or Old Delhi, as it is known today.

**1857: Indian Uprising**
In 1857, Indian soldiers across north India revolted and seized control of major cities which were under British control, including Delhi, Lucknow and Kanpur. Delhi became the focus of the uprising as the

**Bahadur Shah Zafar II**

 Preceding pages **The beautiful Taj Mahal in Agra**

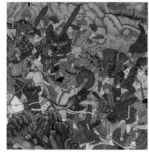

**Painting depicting the Battle of Panipat**

sepoys rallied behind the Mughal emperor, Bahadur Shah Zafar II. The rebellion was quelled and the fighting stopped after months of bitter fighting and Delhi was retaken by the British.

## 1911: Foundation of New Delhi

The capital of British India was moved from Calcutta to Delhi and work began on building the grandiose city of New Delhi under the creative leadership of Edwin Lutyens. The city was inaugurated in 1931 – ironically, the same year the British agreed, in principle, to grant India its independence at a future date.

## 1947: Independence

India was partitioned and became independent. Delhi lost a large proportion of its former Muslim population, while huge numbers of Hindu and Sikh refugees from Pakistan arrived in their place, decisively changing the city's cultural and demographic make up.

## 1984: Assassination of Indira Gandhi and anti-Sikh riots

The assassination of Prime Minister Indira Gandhi (1917–84) by two of her Sikh bodyguards was followed by city-wide communal rioting. Thousands of Sikhs were killed by lynch mobs and their homes set on fire.

## Top 10 Historical Figures

### 1 Qutbuddin Aibak
Turkish slave General Aibak (1150–1210) was the first of the Delhi sultans.

### 2 Alauddin Khilji
Alauddin (r.1296–1316) was perhaps the most brilliant – and certainly the most ruthless – of the Delhi sultans.

### 3 Muhammad bin Tughlaq
The second Tughlaq ruler (1300–51), responsible for moving the capital from Delhi to Daulatabad and back again.

### 4 Babur
The first Mughal emperor (1483–1530). Babur's reign in north India, however, lasted only four years.

### 5 Sher Shah Suri
Formidable Afghan adventurer (1486–1545) who succeeded in wresting power from the second Mughal emperor, Humayun.

### 6 Shah Jahan
Mughal emperor (1592–1666) known for raising monuments including the Taj Mahal.

### 7 Bahadur Shah Zafar II
The last Mughal emperor, Bahadur Shah Zafar II (1775–1862), was the popular figurehead of the 1857 Uprising.

### 8 John Nicholson
A prominent commander (1822–57) in the British Army and the 1857 Uprising.

### 9 Edwin Lutyens
The British architect (1869–1944) who designed much of New Delhi.

### 10 Mohandas K. Gandhi
Eminent leader (1869–1948) of the Indian Independence Movement, assassinated in Delhi after trying to bring peace to the city's warring Hindu and Muslim communities.

Left **Façade of the Red Fort, Shahjahanabad** Right **Qila Rai Pithora walls**

# TOP 10 Cities of Delhi, Old and New

### 1 Indraprastha
The legendary city of Indraprastha, home of the heroic Pandava brothers of the epic *Mahabharata*, is said to have stood on the site now occupied by the Purana Qila. Conclusive evidence is lacking, although archaeological finds have been unearthed here dating back to the 3rd century BC, and an ancient village, Inderpat, stood here until the early 20th century.

### 2 Lal Kot and Qila Rai Pithora
First of the seven cities, Lal Kot was established by a Rajput clan, the Tomars, in 1060. Around a century later, the Tomars became vassals of another Rajput clan, the Chauhans, who extended Lal Kot and renamed it Qila Rai Pithora. Both settlements were largely buried under the Qutb Minar complex *(see pp18–19)*.

### 3 Siri
The second city of Delhi, Siri was built during the reign of Alauddin Khilji *(see p37)*. Little

**Imposing entrance to Jahanpanah**

now remains of it barring a few sections of the walls. More impressive is the water tank Alauddin built nearby at Hauz Khas *(see p96)* to supply water to Siri. It was expanded later by Feroz Shah Tughlaq (r.1351–88). ⊗ *Map V2*

### 4 Tuqhlaqabad
Built during the reign of Ghiyasuddin Tughlaq (r.1320–24), Tuqhlaqabad, the third city of Delhi, was quickly abandoned; according to legend, a sufi saint cursed the place. The city's most impressive features are the massive fortified citadel and ramparts, stretching for over 6 km (4 miles), and the distinctive tomb of Ghiyasuddin himself. A subsidiary fortress, known as Adilabad, stands nearby *(see p97)*.

### 5 Jahanpanah
Delhi's fourth city, Jahanpanah, was built by Muhammad bin Tughlaq *(see p37)* shortly before the eccentric ruler briefly abandoned Delhi for Daulatabad. Two important monuments survive here: the Bijay Mandal, thought to be Tughlaq's palace, and the Begumpuri Masjid *(see p96)*. ⊗ *Map W3*

### 6 Ferozabad
Constructed by Feroz Shah Tughlaq, Ferozabad was the fifth city of Delhi. The principal surviving structure is the walled

→ *There are traditionally held to be seven cities of Delhi – starting with Lal Kot and ending with Shahjahanabad.*

**Ruins of Ferozabad and the Ashokan pillar**

palace complex known as Feroz Shah Kotla *(see p84)*, its crumbling remains topped by one of the city's two Ashokan pillars.

### Purana Qila

Built on the fabled site of Indraprastha, the walled citadel of Purana Qila – the sixth city of Delhi – was begun by the second Mughal Emperor Humayun *(see p16)* and completed by his great rival Sher Shah Suri *(see p37)*. Following Suri's death, Humayun reclaimed his empire and the Purana Qila with it, but died within a year after falling down a steep flight of steps within the complex *(see p89)*.

### Shahjahanabad

Begun by Shah Jahan in 1638 and completed some ten years later, Shahjahanabad (or Old Delhi, as it is now known) was the last of the so-called seven cities of Delhi. It was intended to provide North India with a grand new capital to replace Agra, complete with the Red Fort *(see pp8–9)* and the breath-taking Jama Masjid *(see pp12–13)*.

### New Delhi

Built between 1911 and 1931, the grandiose city of New Delhi represented a conscious attempt by the British to assert their Imperial credentials, featuring showpiece architectural landmarks including India Gate, the Secretariat Buildings and the Rashtrapati Bhavan *(see p17)*. They commissioned British architect Edwin Lutyens *(see p19)*, to create a new city just a stone's throw away from Old Delhi, one that would rival the great cities of the Mughals and the Delhi sultans and thereby legitimize their own, increasingly shaky, hold on the country.

### Gurgaon

Some 15 km (9 miles) south of central Delhi is the satellite city of Gurgaon, in Haryana – the latest in the long series of settlements that have grown up in and around Delhi. A modernistic city of high-rises and shopping malls, Gurgaon is a symbol of the new, affluent, hi-tech India, and has experienced exponential growth over the past decade, attracting a huge number of corporations and wealthy residents away from Delhi.

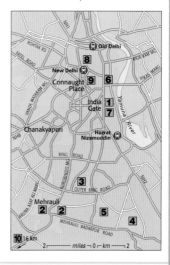

Left **Dussehra celebration** Right **Vintage Car Rally**

# Festivals and Events

**Republic Day Parade**
India's biggest parade celebrates the inauguration of the Indian Constitution on 26 January, 1950. The parade begins at the foot of Raisina Hill *(see p17)* and winds up to the Red Fort, involving a military procession, a cultural parade and a fly-past by the Indian Air Force. ◈ 26 Jan

A plate of
Holi colours

**Beating the Retreat**
Signalling the official end of the Republic Day celebrations, the Beating the Retreat ceremony recalls the old battlefield tradition of soldiers calling a halt to hostilities at the end of the day. It is held at Vijay Chowk *(see p17)* and features an impeccable parade of soldiers accompanied by military bands.

**Summer Theatre Festival, National School of Drama**
Over four weeks each summer, the National School of Drama *(see p50)* hosts a mix of classical and contemporary plays staged by the school's professional repertory company. ◈ May and June • Adm

**Holi**
Vibrant and chaotic, Holi is the traditional Indian spring festival. Bonfires are lit on the eve of the festival, ushering in a day of celebration when people throng the streets throwing coloured powder and water at one another. ◈ Late Feb/early Mar

**Vintage Car Rally**
This event features around a hundred vintage and postwar cars, with their owners dressed in period costume. The rally starts and ends in central Delhi and attracts participants from all over India. ◈ Late Feb/early Mar

**Surajkund Crafts Mela**
Held in Surajkund, about 20 km (12 miles) south of Delhi, this is one of India's biggest craft fairs, showcasing works from all

**Colourful floats at the Republic Day parade**

*For more on Delhi's performing arts venues see **pp50–51**.*

40

**Celebrations during the Surajkund Mela**

over the country, with musicians, dancers and street entertainers creating a carnivalesque atmosphere. ◈ *A fortnight in Feb*

**Phool Walon ki Sair**
The colourful Festival of the Flower-sellers is held in Mehrauli *(see p95)* after the rainy season. The highlight is the procession of flower sellers, led by *shehnai* (a woodwind instrument) players and dancers, during which participants carry floral tributes to the shrine of Qutb Sahib *(see p20)*. ◈ *Usually 3 days in Sep*

**Jahan-e-Khusrau**
This three-day festival of Sufi music commemorates the death of famous Sufi poet and musician Amir Khusrau. Concerts attract leading performers from across the Islamic world. ◈ *Mar*

**Qutb Festival**
A three-day music festival, with concerts held in the Qutb Minar complex, ranging from soulful *qawwali* singers and virtuoso sitar players to young rock bands. ◈ *Nov/Dec*

**The IIC Experience**
Held at the IIC *(see p51)*, this festival hosts a wide range of events from music and dance (Indian and Western) to theatre, film and literature, accompanied by a food festival. ◈ *Mid-Oct*

## Top 10 Religious Festivals

**Maha Shivaratri**
The "Great Night of Shiva" (late Feb/early Mar), marked with fasts and prayers.

**Rama Navami**
Celebration of the birth of Rama (late Mar/early Apr), with continuous readings of the epic *Ramayana*, accompanied by singing and prayers.

**Mahavir Jayanti**
The biggest Jain festival (late Mar/early Apr), celebrating the birth of Mahavir, founder of the religion.

**Buddha Jayanti**
Major religious festival (usually in May), celebrating the birth, enlightenment and death of the Buddha.

**Krishna Janmashtami**
One-day festival (mid-Aug –mid-Sep) celebrating the birth of Krishna with fasting and chanting.

**Ganesh Chaturthi**
Celebrates the birth of Lord Ganesh (ten days between mid-Aug–mid-Sep) with colourful processions.

**Dussehra**
Ten-day festival (mid-Sep –mid-Oct) celebrating the victory of good over evil, including Rama's victory over the demon Ravana and Durga's defeat of Mahishasura.

**Diwali**
Five-day festival of lights (Oct/Nov) in honour of Rama's return from exile, with the lighting of lamps and fireworks.

**Id-ul-Fitr**
Day-long festivities marking the end of the Muslim holy month of Ramadan.

**Guru Purab**
A series of ten Sikh festivals, each celebrating the birth of a Sikh Guru (through the year).

Delhi's Top 10

Left **Ruins in Hauz Khas** Right **Tombs in Lodi Gardens**

# Delhi Sultanate Sights

### Qutb Minar
The defining image of the Delhi Sultanate, the towering Qutb Minar *(see pp18–19)* is a perfect example of the simple but grandiose Sultanate architectural style, intended to symbolize both the military might of the new sultans from Afghanistan and the power of the freshly arrived Islamic faith.

### Quwwat-ul-Islam
The oldest mosque in India, the Quwwat-ul-Islam *(see p18)* is a fascinating study in cultural contrasts. The central courtyard, fashioned out of columns from Hindu and Jain temples that previously stood on this site, has a decidedly Hindu appearance. The magnificent prayer hall screen, however, is a classic work of Islamic architecture covered in Koranic inscriptions.

### Tughlaqabad
Another monumental expression of the power of the Sultanate, the city of Tughlaqabad

**The fortress-like Khirki Masjid**

was built by Ghiyasuddin Tughlaq, founder of the Tughlaq dynasty. The massive fortified citadel – now largely in ruins – was built, astonishingly, in just two years *(see p97)*.

### Tomb of Ghiyasuddin Tughlaq
This simple yet striking red tomb is the final resting place of one of medieval India's most powerful rulers. The tomb is an almost windowless structure with sloping sides set within a small fortified compound. ⌾ *Map X3 • Tughlaqabad*

### Lal Gumbad
Built for local Sufi saint Kabiruddin Aulia in 1397, the Lal Gumbad is very similar to the earlier tomb of Ghiyasuddin Tughlaq – a minimalist cube of red sandstone, almost devoid of extraneous decoration. Tughlaq architecture at its most memorably simple and austere. ⌾ *Map V2 • Panchshila Park South, off Gamal Abdel Nasser Marg • Open 24 hrs*

### Khirki Masjid
Another superbly atmospheric Tughlaq-era mosque built in the 1370s, the Khirki Masjid looks more like a fortress than a place of worship. ⌾ *Map V3 • Press Enclave Road • Open daily sunrise–sunset*

### Begumpuri Masjid
The finest of the various Sultanate-era mosques scattered about the city, the Begumpuri Masjid is a perfect example of the

There were 36 Delhi sultans in all, representing five separate dynasties.

The double-storeyed *madrasa* at Hauz Khas

austere and monumental style favoured by the Tughlaq Dynasty. The simple mosque is raised, fortress-like, above the surrounding streets, centred on a huge courtyard, with a massive gateway above the central prayer hall.

### Hauz Khas
The lake in Hauz Khas was built by Alauddin Khilji in 1304 to supply water to his new city at Siri, although most of the pavilions around it were added half a century later by Feroz Shah Tughlaq, who is buried here.

### Feroz Shah Kotla
All that remains of the great city of Ferozabad *(see p38–9)* is a walled enclosure containing the fragmentary remains of a royal palace, mosque and other structures. The most eye-catching feature here is the Ashokan column, perched atop the citadel, dating from the 3rd century BC.

### Lodi Gardens
The delicately constructed octagonal tombs of Muhammad Shah, Sikander Lodi and other sultans are dotted throughout the idyllic Lodi Gardens *(see pp24–5)*. Their relatively small scale (and light style) serve to illustrate the declining fortunes of the Sayyid and Lodi dynasties.

## Top 10 Delhi Sultans

**Qutbuddin Aibak**
The first Delhi sultan, Aibak (1150–1210) founded the so-called Slave Dynasty.

**Iltutmish**
Son of Aibak, Iltutmish (r.1211–36) extended the territory of the Sultanate from Punjab to Bengal.

**Razia Sultan**
Iltutmish's daughter (r.1236–40) and India's only female leader until Indira Gandhi, seven centuries later.

**Alauddin Khilji**
Alauddin (r.1296–1316) was the most illustrious ruler of the Khilji dynasty.

**Ghiyasuddin Tughlaq**
Ghiyasuddin (r.1320–24) founded the Tughlaq dynasty after displacing the Khiljis.

**Muhammad bin Tughlaq**
Eccentric ruler (r.1325–51) who tried to relocate the capital from Delhi to Daulatabad but later moved it back.

**Feroz Shah Tughlaq**
Feroz Shah Tughlaq (r.1351–88) tried to repair the damage inflicted on the Sultanate by his predecessor.

**Khizr Khan**
Khizr Khan (r.1414–21) took advantage of the power vacuum created by Timur's invasion in 1398 to establish the Sayyid Dynasty (1414–51).

**Buhlul Lodi**
Punjab governor (r.1451–89) who seized power from the Sayyids, establishing the last of the Sultanate's five dynasties, the Lodi Dynasty.

**Sikander Lodi**
Sikander Lodi (r.1489–1517) was the last effective Delhi sultan. His son, Ibrahim Lodi (r.1517–26), was overthrown by the great Babur, the first of the Mughals.

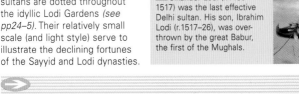

Left **Imposing entrance to Purana Qila** Right **Jamali-Kamali Masjid, Mehrauli**

# ⓾ Mughal Delhi Sights

### ⓵ Jamali-Kamali Masjid

Completed in 1536 during the first period of Humayun's reign (see p15), the simple but elegant Jamali-Kamali Masjid is Delhi's finest example of early-Mughal architecture (see p20).

**Detail of Bu Halima**

### ⓶ Purana Qila

The oldest major Mughal monument in Delhi, the Purana Qila was begun by Humayun and completed by his Afghan successor, Sher Shah Suri (see p37) after he had driven his rival into exile in Persia (see p89).

### ⓷ Humayun's Tomb

Humayun's Tomb exemplifies many of the design elements which were to become standard features of the Mughal style, including the use of red sandstone with marble inlay work,

**The grand façade of the Red Fort**

enormous *iwans* and the setting of the entire tomb within a lovely Persian-style *charbagh* garden (see pp14–15).

### ⓸ Khan-i-Khanan

The imposing tomb of Abdur Rahim, who served as prime minister to Akbar but later fell foul of Jahangir, is now dilapidated, but still impressive. It is clearly modelled on the nearby Humayun's Tomb, though its shape hints at the later Taj Mahal (see p90).

### ⓹ Nizamuddin

The interesting religious complex at Nizamuddin is home to a number of Mughal structures, including the tombs of Ataga Khan (1562) and the saint Nizamuddin Aulia (1325), both built during the reign of Akbar (see p90).

### ⓺ Red Fort

Despite suffering considerable damage during the 1857 Uprising and after, the Red Fort remains a treasure trove of Mughal architectural styles, with imposing gateways, formal gardens and a sequence of royal pavilions strung out along the ramparts (see pp8–9).

### ⓻ Jama Masjid

India's largest mosque, Shah Jahan's Jama Masjid is the epitome of Mughal religious architecture: a dramatically simple

For a description of the great Mughal monuments of Agra see pp32–3.

Exquisite façade of Safdarjung's Tomb

composition of massive arches, domes and minarets, towering high above the crowded streets of Old Delhi *(see pp12–13)*.

### Safdarjung's Tomb

Safdarjung's Tomb is the last major Mughal mausoleum in Delhi and generally reckoned to exemplify the creative decline that set in following the demise of Shah Jahan, though its fanciful façades and interior, lend it a certain kitsch charm, entirely its own *(see p90)*.

### Zinat ul Masjid

Dating from the reign of Aurangzeb, this neglected architectural gem is a perfect example of Mughal architecture in miniature – like a scaled-down version of the Jama Masjid, with a trio of marbled onion domes topping the beautifully proportioned prayer hall below *(see p82)*.

### Zafar Mahal

Built by the Mughal Emperor Akbar Shah II in the 18th century, and the last major monument of Mughal India, the Zafar Mahal summer palace is a quaint exercise in architectural nostalgia by an increasingly powerless, and soon to be extinguished, dynasty *(see p21)*.

## Top 10 Mughal Design Features

**1 Red Sandstone and White Marble**
A classic Mughal combination: façades of red sandstone decorated with bands of white marble inlay.

**2 Iwans**
These huge central arches provide a focus on the façades of tombs and mosques.

**3 Cusped Arches**
Staple of Mughal architecture, derived from Rajasthani and Bengali styles.

**4 Pietra Dura**
A hallmark of the Shah Jahan-era style, where colourful gemstones are embedded in white marble to create floral or abstract designs.

**5 Jalis**
Delicately carved marble or sandstone screens, often used to enclose tombs.

**6 Tilework**
Derived from Persia, this technique uses coloured tiles (usually, but not exclusively, blue) to decorate domes, window frames and façades.

**7 Charbagh Gardens**
Persian-style gardens, divided by a network of water channels into four quadrants.

**8 Domes**
Distinctive Persian-style onion domes, often crowned with dramatic finials, an element from Hindu traditions.

**9 Chattris**
Small, domed pavilions supported on four pillars, common in Hindu architecture and used on the eaves and minarets of Mughal buildings.

**10 Jharokas**
These distinctive balconied windows, often richly carved, are another classic Hindu feature widely adopted in Mughal architecture.

Left **Brass statue, Chawri Bazaar** Centre **Guliyan Bazaar** Right **Posters in Nai Sarak market**

# 🔟 Bazaars of Old Delhi

**1 Dariba Kalan**
Dating back to the days of Shah Jahan, "The Street of the Incomparable Pearl" is Old Delhi's foremost jewellery bazaar, with shops selling an array of precious stones and metals including an especially good selection of silverware as well as traditional attar-based *itr* perfumes. 🖎 *Map H3*

**2 Kinari Bazaar**
Just off Dariba Kalan, the shops of Kinari Bazaar are famous for their wedding paraphernalia and other "fancy goods" – garlands of fake flowers and banknotes, reams of gold and silver tinsel, bridal veils, turbans for grooms and huge quantities of sparkly costume jewellery, as well as items used in the *Ramayana* performances which are staged all over the city during the festival of Dussehra. 🖎 *Map G3*

**3 Guliyan Bazaar**
Stretching around the northwestern side of Jama Masjid, this is the place to come to stock up on fireworks for a wedding or a festival, with shops filled with piles of brightly col-oured boxes full of rockets, fire-crackers and other things that go bang. 🖎 *Map H4*

**4 Car Parts Bazaar**
Sprawling around the south and west sides of the Jama Masjid, this is one of Old Delhi's more workaday bazaars selling mechanical bits and bobs. Visitors will find everything from wheels, doors, hubcaps, panels and entire engines – a surreal sight in the shadow of the beautiful mosque. 🖎 *Map H3*

**5 Khari Baoli**
Said to be the biggest spice market in Asia, Khari Baoli is one of Old Delhi's most absorbing

**Wedding accessories strung between shops in Kinari Bazaar**

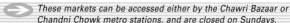

*These markets can be accessed either by the Chawri Bazaar or Chandni Chowk metro stations, and are closed on Sundays.*

An array of spices in Khari Baoli

western end of the road specialize in lovely brass and copper ornaments. ◈ Map G4

### Meena Bazaar
**8** Sprawling across the steps around and below the Jama Masjid is Old Delhi's foremost religious bazaar, with stalls selling prayer rugs, framed Koranic inscriptions, pictures of Mecca and other Muslim shrines, Islamic-style clocks and other religious bric-a-brac *(see p12)*.

### Katra Neel
**9** Just off Chandni Chowk, immediately west of the Town Hall, this fascinating labyrinth of tiny alleyways is cluttered with shops festooned with all manner of ladies' clothing – shawls, salwar kameezes, saris and a wide variety of textiles, such as brocades from Benarasi, silk and voile. ◈ Map G3

An array of spices in Khari Baoli

sights. Lively and congested in equal measure, it is lined by shops crammed with all kinds of spices, pulses, dried fruits and other edibles. Innumerable barrow boys fight their way through the crowds, deftly avoiding sacks of produce that lie stacked up in great piles in the street. ◈ Map F3

### Nai Sarak
**6** This street, created by the British in 1857 (hence the name, meaning "New Street") cuts across the heart of the old city. It is now Old Delhi's main book market, with shops selling dog-eared, second-hand school and college textbooks and technical tomes. ◈ Map G3

### Chawri Bazaar
**7** Old Delhi's stationery bazaar is devoted to shops selling writing paper, greetings cards (including an area dedicated entirely to the printing of wedding cards) and other paper products. Paper here is sold by weight and is very cheap. Shops at the

*Jutis* from Ballimaran

### Ballimaran
**10** The Chandni Chowk end of this long Old Delhi thoroughfare is the place to go to for shoes. It has every conceivable variety of footwear, from humble plastic *chappals* (flip-flops) to finely crafted traditional Indian *jutis* (slippers), hand-stitched in leather. ◈ Map G3

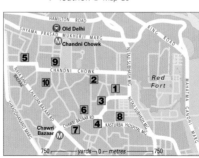

Left **Graves in Nicholson's Cemetery** Right **Arch of the Lal Darwaza**

# Monuments of the 1857 Uprising

### Fatehpuri Masjid
The Fatehpuri Masjid was a hotbed of nationalist sentiment and religious fervour during the 1857 Uprising. The British responded by sacking the mosque and selling it to a local business-man, although two decades later they bought it back and returned it to Delhi's Muslim community. A number of Indian soldiers killed in the uprising lie buried in the courtyard *(see p11)*.

### Magazine
Now marooned on a traffic island in the middle of Sham Nath Marg, the small British magazine was at the heart of fighting on the first day of hostilities in Delhi. Finding themselves surrounded by enemy Indian sepoys, the British troops stationed inside the magazine decided to blow it up rather than allow its stock of arms and ammunition to fall into Indian hands. The explosion killed around 400 sepoys and onlook-ers, although, miraculously, six of the magazine's nine British defenders survived. *Map H2 • Sham Nath Marg • Kashmiri Gate Metro*

### British Residency
The old Neo-Classical British Residency was built around the ruins of a Mughal library erected by Dara Shikoh (1615–59), son of Shah Jahan. It is now home to the Archaeology Department of the Guru Gobind Singh Indraprastha University. *Map H2 • Sham Nath Marg • Kashmiri Gate Metro*

### Northern Ridge
North of Old Delhi, the northern extension of the Aravalli Range forms a long, low ridge. This is where refugees from Delhi gathered after the outbreak of the 1857 Uprising, and where British military forces gathered over the following months, surviving repeated sepoy attacks before launching their assault to recapture the city *(see p84)*.

**Flagstaff Tower on the Northern Ridge**

### Flagstaff Tower
The Flagstaff Tower, at the northern end of the Northern Ridge, was originally built in 1828 as a British signalling post. It served as a shelter for civilians fleeing the city after the outbreak of hostilities during the uprising when dozens of refugees sought shelter within its tiny, airless interior. *Map B4 • Magazine Road, Northern Ridge • Vidhan Sabha Metro*

### St James' Church
This beautiful Colonial-era church holds a number of memo-rials to British civilians killed in

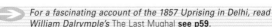 *For a fascinating account of the 1857 Uprising in Delhi, read William Dalrymple's* The Last Mughal **see p59.**

Delhi during the 1857 Uprising. It also contains a memorial to the Reverend Midgeley John Jennings, then chaplain of Delhi, whose high-handed Christian evangelizing did much to enflame local religious sensibilities, and who was killed in the Red Fort during the first hours of the revolt *(see p82)*.

### 7 Kashmiri Gate

Now dwarfed by the vast new Kashmiri Gate Metro, this modest little Mughal-era gateway witnessed the most bitter fighting of the entire uprising when British troops stormed the gate in order to force a route into the rebel-held city. A plaque at the rear commemorates those killed in the assault. ⚑ Map G2 • Sham Nath Marg • Kashmiri Gate Metro

### 8 Nicholson's Cemetery

Tucked away in Old Delhi is this atmospheric and rambling Colonial-era cemetery. Beautifully restored in 2006, Nicholson's Cemetery is home to the graves of hundreds of India's early European inhabitants. Among the many graves, the most famous is that of Brigadier-General John Nicholson *(see p37)*, one of the key British figures in the history of the 1857 Uprising, who was killed during the recapture of Delhi *(see p84)*.

### 9 Lal Darwaza

The red sandstone Lal Darwaza (also known as the Khooni Darwaza, or Bloody Gate) marks the site of one of the most notorious episodes of the uprising when British officer William Hodson summarily executed Mirza Mughal, Kizr Sultan and Abu Bakr, sons and grandson, respectively, of the last Mughal Emperor

**Mutiny Monument, Northern Ridge**

Bahadur Shah Zafar II *(see p37)*.
⚑ Map Q4 • Mathura Road • Pragati Maidan Metro

### 10 Mutiny Monument

At the southern end of the Northern Ridge, this grandiose Gothic-style Victorian monument, built in 1863, commemorates the British soldiers (and "native" troops in British employ) killed during the uprising, with panels listing the names, ranks and numbers of military fatalities. An additional panel, added in 1972, offers an Indian perspective on the events described. ⚑ Map E1 • Rani Jhansi Road • Pulbangash Metro

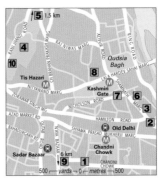

Left **Mask from Kerala, Sangeet Natak Akademi** Centre **Folk dancers** Right *Qawwali* **singers**

# 🔟 Performing Arts Venues

### 1 Kamani Auditorium
The Kamani Auditorium is one of the city's leading venues for classical music and dance, attracting leading performers from across the country. ✎ *Map Q1*
• *Mandi House, 1, Copernicus Marg*
• *4350 3351 • Mandi House Metro*
• *www.kamaniauditorium.org*

### 2 Shri Ram Center for Performing Arts
Established in 1975, this is an important theatrical venue, with its own outstanding repertory company, staging a range of interesting productions including musical, traditional and experimental theatre. ✎ *Map Q1 • 4, Safdar Hashmi Marg • 2371 4307 • Mandi House Metro • www.shriramcenterart.org*

### 3 National School of Drama
The National School of Drama (NSD), established in 1959, is the country's leading academy for aspiring actors. Productions are staged by current students and the school's excellent professional repertory company.
✎ *Map Q1 • Bahawalpur House,*
*1, Bhagwan Das Road • 2338 2821*
• *Mandi House Metro • www.nsd.gov.in*

### 4 Sangeet Natak Akademi
Opened in 1953, this is one of the country's foremost performing arts venues, with perhaps the finest open-air theatre in the capital. It also has an important library and a gallery showcasing traditional musical instruments, masks and puppets. ✎ *Map P1*
• *Rabindra Bhavan, 35, Feroz Shah Road*
• *2338 7246 • Mandi House Metro*
• *www.sangeetnatak.org*

### 5 India Habitat Centre
One of Delhi's state-of-the-art performing arts venues, hosting regular music, dance and cultural events such as art-house

**A traditional folk play at the National School of Drama**

Tickets for events in Delhi are usually excellent value, and rarely more than Rs.200.

film screenings and talks.
⊗ *Map P6* • *Lodi Road* • *2468 2001*
• *www.indiahabitat.org*

**India International Centre**
Besides regular music, dance and theatrical performances, the India International Centre (IIC) hosts exhibitions and talks attracting leading cultural personalities from Salman Rushdie to Noam Chomsky. It also hosts a cinema club with art-house film screenings. ⊗ *Map P6* • *40, Max Mueller Marg* • *2461 9431* • *www.iicdelhi.nic.in*

**Triveni Kala Sangam**
This cultural centre houses a range of venues, including galleries, an auditorium and an open-air theatre, staging regular music and dance performances.
⊗ *Map G7* • *205, Tansen Marg* • *2371 8833* • *Mandi House Metro*

**Nizamuddin**
The fascinating religious enclave of Nizamuddin is Delhi's most atmospheric venue for impromptu music, with nightly performances of ecstatic *qawwali* singing around the shrine of Nizamuddin Aulia, the famous Sufi saint *(see p90)*.

**Parsi Anjuman Hall**
Home to the popular Dances of India show (daily at 6:45pm), featuring a mixed programme of classical and folk dances. ⊗ *Map H5* • *Bahadur Shah Zafar Marg* • *2623 4689* • *Pragati Maidan Metro*

**Siri Fort**
The extensive Siri Fort Cultural Complex boasts three auditoriums (the largest seating almost 2,000 people), staging a range of big-name events, particularly Indian classical music concerts, dance and film. ⊗ *Map V2* • *Khel Gaon Marg* • *2649 3370*

## Top 10 Forms of Indian Classical Music

**1 Raga**
The system of modes underlying most Indian classical music; also used to describe extended pieces employing the traditional *alap–jor–jhala–gat* structure.

**2 Padam**
Light classical love songs in the Carnatic tradition, often sung during Bharatnatyam dance performances.

**3 Khayal**
An elaborate and often virtuoso style of North Indian singing, based on extended improvisation on short songs.

**4 Ghazal**
Persian-derived classical song form, often using lyrics by Urdu poets and generally performed by male vocalists.

**5 Thumri**
A type of love song, usually performed by female singers in a Lucknow dialect of Hindi known as Braj Bhasa.

**6 Qawaali**
Sufi devotional music, with ecstatic singing accompanied by harmoniums and drums.

**7 Dhrupad**
One of the oldest and most austere forms of Hindustani vocal music, said to have developed from the chanting of Vedic hymns and mantras.

**8 Kriti**
The major vocal genre of Carnatic music, in three parts, and with a religious theme.

**9 Tarana**
North Indian vocal genre involving the rapid singing of meaningless syllables.

**10 Varnam**
Form of Carnatic vocal music and a traditional concert-opener, designed to bring out the qualities of an underlying raga.

Left **St James' Church** Centre **Meena Bazaar, Jama Masjid** Right **Akshardham Temple**

# Places of Worship

### Jama Masjid
Despite the exodus of many of the old city's Muslims during the Partition in 1947, Delhi's spectacular Jama Masjid remains an important centre for Islamic worship, particularly during communal prayers, when it fills with worshippers *(see pp12–13)*.

### Baha'i Temple
India's answer to the Sydney Opera House, this remarkable building – an abstract composition inspired by the shape of an unfurling lotus flower – was built for the Baha'i faith. Founded by 19th-century Persian visionary Baha'u'llah, Baha'i stresses the connections between the major world religions and now claims over five million followers worldwide *(see p95)*.

**Façade of the Baha'i Temple**

### St James' Church
Easily the most attractive church in the city, this Colonial gem was built by the legendary Anglo-Indian soldier James Skinner (1778–1841). Barred from serving in the British army due to his mixed race, Skinner established his own irregular cavalry regiment, the celebrated Skinner's Horse, which forms a part of the Indian army to this day *(see p82)*.

### Akshardham Temple
This gargantuan modern temple was built in honour of the sage Bhagwan Shri Swaminarayan (1781–1830), who left his birthplace in Uttar Pradesh at the age of 11 and walked for seven years and 12,000 km (7,456 miles) before establishing an ashram in Gujarat. From here, he preached a message of non-violence and spiritual unity, attracting Hindu followers as well as Muslims and Zoroastrians *(see p89)*.

### Gurudwara Bangla Sahib
Built in 1783 in honour of the eighth Sikh Guru Har Krishan, this is the city's largest Sikh temple. The guru visited Delhi in 1664 during a cholera and smallpox epidemic, tending to the sick and offering them fresh water from the *sarovar* (lake) on the site, which is still believed to possess medicinal properties *(see p76)*.

**The sanctum in Gurudwara Bangla Sahib**

*Delhi is religiously very diverse, with Muslims, Sikhs, Jains, a few Christians and Parsis living alongside the Hindu majority.*

### Nizamuddin
One of the most magical places in Delhi, the wonderfully atmospheric religious complex of Nizamuddin grew up around the revered *dargah* (Muslim shrine) of the Chishti Sufi saint Nizamuddin Aulia. Among the cluster of structures now surrounding the saint's tomb are the Jamat Khana Masjid (1325) and the graves of the famous poet Amir Khusrau (1253–1325) and Princess Jahanara, Shah Jahan's daughter *(see p90)*.

**Women at prayer, Nizamuddin**

### Lakshmi Narayan Mandir
This eye-catching modern Hindu temple was commissioned by billionaire industrialist R.D. Birla and consecrated in 1938 by Gandhi – one of the first temples in India open to everyone, irrespective of caste. The bright and spacious interior is centred on a shrine to Lakshmi and her consort Narayan (Vishnu), flanked by images of Durga and a meditating Shiva *(see p75)*.

### Lal Mandir
This Jain temple is one of the city's most important and a notable Old Delhi landmark. Topped by a cluster of towers, made of red Kota stone, it has a richly painted interior, full of diminutive marble images of various Jain gurus in glass cases. Next to the temple is a small "bird hospital" where birds are fed and cared for – evidence of the profound respect which the Jain religion has for all forms of life *(see p10)*.

### Zinat ul Masjid
Popularly known as the Ghata (Cloud) Masjid, this beautiful building was commissioned by Aurangzeb's daughter Zinat ul Nisa and completed in 1707. It is the only one of the city's later Mughal monuments to rival the earlier creations of Shah Jahan *(see p82)*.

### Begumpuri Masjid
Built in the 1340s by Muhammad bin Tughlaq as part of his city of Jahanpanah, this little-visited but atmospheric mosque is one of the finest in Delhi. The mosque is centred on a huge courtyard surrounded by domed arcades, with a fortress-like gateway leading into the prayer hall – a perfect example of Tughlaq architecture at its rugged and imposing best *(see p96)*.

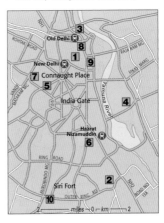

Left **Indira Gandhi Memorial Museum** Centre **Nehru Memorial Museum** Right **Rail Museum**

# 🔟 Museums and Galleries

*Saraswati*, NGMA

### National Museum
The National Museum is an obligatory first stop on any tour of Delhi's museums with a superb array of exhibits covering every epoch in the country's history, ranging from priceless Harappan artifacts through to Chola bronzes and Mughal miniatures *(see pp26–9)*.

### Jawaharlal Nehru Memorial Museum
The Teen Murti House, formerly called Flagstaff House, was built in 1930 as the residence of the British military commander-in-chief and later became home to India's first Prime Minister Jawaharlal Nehru (1889–1964). There are a few photographs and

newspaper cuttings on display, but the main attraction is the house itself, including rooms left exactly as they were when Nehru lived here *(see p76)*.

### Indira Gandhi Memorial Museum
This is the former home of Indira Gandhi (1917–84), who was assassinated in the garden here by two of her Sikh bodyguards. The absorbing exhibits include personal belongings and photos, plus a section devoted to her son Rajiv (1944–91), including the shoes he was wearing when he was killed by Tamil separatists in 1991 *(see p74)*.

### Gandhi Smriti
Formerly known as Birla House, this Neo-Classical mansion is where Gandhi (1869–1948) spent the last 144 days of his life. Displays include a touching collection of the Mahatma's personal belongings, including the watch he was wearing when he was assasinated, which stopped at the moment of his death *(see p74)*.

**Gandhi and his spinning wheel, Gandhi Smriti Museum**

### National Gandhi Museum
The city's second Gandhi museum is close to the spot at Raj Ghat where his body was cremated. Exhibits include personal effects and

 *Note that many of Delhi's museums are closed on Monday.*

photographs, plus six telephones on which one can listen to his speeches in Hindi and English.
◈ Map J5 • Raj Ghat • 2331 1793 • Open Tue–Sat, and on Sun 9:30am–5:30pm
• www.gandhimuseum.org

### National Philatelic Museum
Heaven for stamp enthusiasts, the National Philatelic Museum holds a copy of every Indian stamp produced since Independence (around 1,700 issues), as well as a selection of international stamps and the personal belongings of a mid-19th-century postman (see p76).

### Crafts Museum
Another of Delhi's must-see cultural attractions, showcasing a variety of artifacts inspired by the country's indigenous folk art traditions. Exhibits range from detailed ivory carvings to a set of traditional buildings from around India erected in the grounds outside (see pp22–3).

### National Gallery of Modern Art (NGMA)
Relocated to a new, purpose-built structure in 2009, the NGMA houses works dating from 1857 to the present. Among them are a good selection of miniatures, East India Company Art and works by classic Orientalist artists such as Thomas Daniell, as well as a collection of works by the eclectic Bengali artist Nandalal Bose (see p76).

### National Rail Museum
India's love affair with the railway is celebrated in this fine

Painting by Thomas Daniell, NGMA

museum containing assorted antique steam engines and opulent carriages, including those once belonging to the maharajas of Mysore and Baroda, and the Prince of Wales (see p91).

### Sulabh International Museum of Toilets
Although this museum may sound like a joke, it has quite a serious purpose being part of the neo-Gandhian Sulabh International Movement, which aims to promote public hygiene, with many displays on lavatorial habits.
◈ Map A5 • Mahavir Enclave, Palam Dabri Marg • 2503 1518 • Uttam Nagar East Metro • Open Mon–Sat 10am–5pm
• www.sulabhtoiletmuseum.org

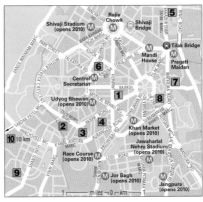

Left **Raj-era statues at Coronation Park** Right **Buddha Jayanti Park**

# Parks and Gardens

### Lodi Gardens
Arguably the most attractive gardens in Delhi, boasting idyllic lawns and shady patches of woodland dotted with the imposing tombs of assorted Lodi and Sayyid nobles *(see pp24–5)*.

### Mughal Gardens
Tucked away in the sprawling grounds of Rashtrapati Bhavan, the Mughal Gardens are open to the public only for a month in spring, but are worth a visit. Designed by Lutyens in a blend of Mughal and English styles, they boast many rare species of flora, including 250 varieties of rose and 60 types of bougainvillea *(see p17)*.

### Hauz Khas Deer Park
Close to the old tank and monuments of Hauz Khas Village *(see p96)*, the beautiful Hauz Khas Deer Park is an area of peaceful, shady woodland, complete with pens of spotted deer, roving peacocks and abundant bird life.

**Beautiful paths in Qudsia Bagh**

### Qudsia Bagh
North of Old Delhi lies Qudsia Bagh created in 1748 as a royal pleasure park by Qudsia Begum (1801–81), wife of Mughal Emperor Muhammad Shah. Little survives of the park's original buildings apart from a florid gateway, and a delicate little mosque at the garden's southeastern end *(see p84)*.

### Raj Ghat
These extensive gardens are best known as the place where the funeral rites of modern India's most important leaders took place, including Mahatma Gandhi, Indira Gandhi, Rajiv Gandhi and Jawaharlal Nehru, each of whom is commemorated with a monument *(see p81)*.

### Buddha Jayanti Park
Hemmed in amidst the woodland of the Ridge west of New Delhi, this beautiful park was created in 1993 to mark the 2,500th anniversary of the Buddha's enlightenment. A gilded Buddha statue sits within the park. Map K2 • Vandemataram Marg • Open daily 5am–7pm

### Talkatora Gardens
Right behind the Rashtrapati Bhavan, these 18th-century gardens remain one of central Delhi's most popular parks, particularly pretty in spring when their colourful shrubs burst into life. Map L2 • Mother Teresa Road • Open daily sunrise–sunset

*Almost all Delhi's parks and gardens are free to enter.*

Stone pathways in the Garden of Five Senses

### Nehru Park

Covering almost 80 acres, Nehru Park is one of the most popular retreats in South Delhi, with spacious lawns and a swimming pool. The park also hosts concerts of Indian classical music every Sunday morning.
Ⓢ *Map L6 • Panchsheel Road, Chanyakapuri • Open daily sunrise–sunset*

### Garden of Five Senses

Delhi's most unusual and artistic garden, dotted with sculptures. The gardens themselves are divided into differently landscaped areas with sensory themes such as the "Trail of Fragrance" and "Colour Gardens".
Ⓢ *Map V3 • Said-ul-Ajaib village, near Mahavirsthal on the Mehrauli–Badarpur Road • Open daily 8am–9pm • Adm*

### Coronation Park

Some 10 km (6 miles) north of Connaught Place, this was the site of the three great British Durbars of 1887, 1903 and 1911. Following Independence, the park was used as a dumping ground for assorted Raj-era statues that once graced the city, most notably an imposing statue of King George V that once stood in front of India Gate.
Ⓢ *Map B4 • Burari Road near Nirankari Sarovar • Open sunrise–sunset*

## Top 10 Indian Trees

**1 Indian Temple Tree (Plumeria)**
Popularly known as Frangipani, this is one of the most common Indian flowering shrubs, producing huge white flowers.

**2 Jacaranda**
A flowering tree, which explodes in spring into a distinctive purple blossom.

**3 Pipul (Ficus Religiosa)**
A species of banyan fig, and Buddhism's sacred tree (also known as the Bodhi tree).

**4 Indian Laburnam (Cassia Fistula)**
A shrub with Ayurvedic properties that bursts into yellow flowers in late spring.

**5 Gulmohar (Delonix Regia)**
Easily recognizable by its distinctive fern-like leaves and red flowers.

**6 Red Silk Cotton Tree (Bombax Ceiba)**
Attractive ornamental tree, especially pretty in spring when it is covered in red flowers, with no leaves.

**7 Jamun (Syzygium Cumini)**
Evergreen tree known for its large purple berries and mentioned in the *Ramayana*.

**8 Kachnar (Bauhinia Variegata)**
A popular ornamental tree, with large, scented, pink or white flowers.

**9 Flame of the Forest (Butea Monosperma)**
Also known as the *dhak* tree, this flowering species has curved, orange flowers.

**10 Neem (Azadirachta Indica)**
Common South Asian tree renowned for its medicinal properties; hence its popular description as the "village pharmacy".

Left *Delhi: A Novel* Centre **William Dalrymple signing books** Right *Delhi: Adventures in a Megacity*

# Top 10 Delhi-inspired Books

### 1 City of Djinns (William Dalrymple)

A beautifully written portrait of Delhi's multi-layered personality. Particularly strong on the city's history, interspersed with richly comic snapshots of the modern city.

### 2 Delhi: Adventures in a Megacity (Sam Miller)

This entertaining eye-witness account of contemporary Delhi follows a spiralling perambulation through the city, from the centre of Connaught Place out into the suburbs, with descriptions of the many people and places encountered on his journey.

### 3 Scoop-wallah: Life on a Delhi Daily (Justine Hardy)

An engrossing account of a year spent by English journalist Justine Hardy as a reporter for the *Indian Express*, offering fascinating insights into the city's complex social fabric, from the lives of slum dwellers to the Westernized airs of the aristocratic elite.

### 4 Clear Light of Day (Anita Desai)

This is Anita Desai's most obviously autobiographical work, centred on the contrasting stories of two sisters from Old Delhi – one of whom leaves the city and

*White Tiger* by Aravind Adiga

the other who remains – and their subsequent reunion.

### 5 White Tiger (Aravind Adiga)

Booker Prize-winning debut novel by Chennai-born Aravind Adiga, partly set in Delhi, relating the murderous career of anti-hero Balram Halwai, with insights into contemporary Indian society en route.

### 6 Delhi: A Novel (Kushwant Singh)

An off-beat and engaging novel by one of India's foremost living writers. Historical snapshots of the city through the ages – culminating in the anti-Sikh riots of 1984 – are interspersed with a secondary narrative about a journalist and his passionate relationship with a *hijra* (eunuch).

### 7 New Delhi: Making of a Capital (Malvika Singh)

This beautifully produced coffee-table book offers fascinating insights into the creation of the capital of British Imperial India, bringing together many original documents and photographs to light for the first time as well as highlighting the fierce battles between architects Edwin Lutyens and Herbert Baker over the course of this mammoth undertaking.

 *There are several excellent bookshops around Connaught Place, including Amrit Book Company (block N-21).*

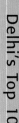

### 8 Twilight in Delhi (Ahmed Ali)

Classic novel by Delhi-born Muslim author Ahmed Ali which paints a beautiful portrait of the city at the beginning of the 20th century – an elegiac lament for the city's rapidly disappearing Mughal traditions in the face of the Colonial and European cultural onslaught.

### 9 Delhi Noir (edited by Hirsh Sawhney)

An absorbing journey into the dark underbelly of the capital, comprising 14 stories by authors, including Irwin Allan Sealy, Ruchir Joshi and Tabish Khair, conjuring up a world of sex, crime and vigilante rickshaw drivers.

### 10 The Last Mughal (William Dalrymple)

A landmark study of the history of the 1857 Uprising. Dalrymple draws on a wealth of unpublished contemporary source material, offering the most even-handed and objective account of the conflict yet published in English.

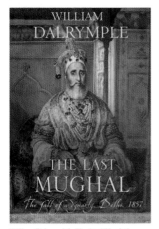

William Dalrymple's *The Last Mughal*

## Top 10 Delhi Films

### 1 Woh Chokri (1994)
A bleak portrait of contemporary Indian life, depicting the struggles of an abandoned mother and her illegitimate daughter.

### 2 Fire (1996)
A controversial tale of a lesbian affair between two Delhi wives.

### 3 Monsoon Wedding (2001)
Mira Nair's marvellously evocative portrait of Delhi, combining deft social comedy with stunning cinematography.

### 4 Kabhi Khushi Kabhie Gham (2001)
Filmed in India and London, this box office hit depicts the vicissitudes of a divided family, brought to life by a star cast.

### 5 Rang de Basanti (2006)
An influential film by Rakeysh Omprakash Mehra about five young men trying to expose political corruption.

### 6 Fanaa (2006)
The story of a blind Kashmiri college student who falls in love, fatefully, with a Kashmiri terrorist.

### 7 Chak De (2007)
Shahrukh Khan stars as disgraced Indian hockey player Kabir Khan.

### 8 Delhi 6 (2009)
A Rakeysh Omprakash Mehra film depicting the lives and loves of an eclectic array of Old Delhi characters.

### 9 Dev D (2009)
Clever, contemporary reworking of the classic Bengali movie *Devdas*.

### 10 Chandni Chowk to China (2009)
Set in India and China and starring Akshay Kumar as Sidhu, a Delhi vegetable chopper turned Kung-fu hero.

The beautifully illuminated India Gate

# Walks Around Delhi

### 1 Lodi Gardens

This beautifully landscaped park is a great place for a walk. Start at any of the gates and stroll around the evocative Lodi and Sayyid period monuments. Don't miss the three-acre butterfly park, complete with a pretty lily pool (see pp24–5).

Bonsai at Lodi Gardens

### 2 Mehrauli Archaeological Park

Enter the Qutb complex via the main ticketed entrance and take time wandering around the crumbling ruins. For the park, go out of the main gate and down the Mehrauli-Gurgaon road to the entrance next to the roadside flower market (see p20).

### 3 Mehrauli Village

Start from the Mehrauli parking lot, near the bus terminal. Before you end at One Style Mile, one of the city's hippest shopping areas, stop by at Adham Khan's Tomb, Zafar Mahal and Jahaz Mahal from where you can climb on to its roof to gaze around the area (see pp20–21).

Detail, Quli Khan's Tomb, Mehrauli

### 4 Hauz Khas

Begin at the entrance of Deer Park; from here the deer herd and reservoir can be found at the end of many winding, tree-lined paths. Adjacent is the quaint Hauz Khas Village where you can stop for a meal and some excellent boutique shopping. Explore the crumbling ruins at the end of the market (see p96).

### 5 Chandni Chowk

Start at the Lal Mandir opposite the Red Fort, next door to the Gauri Shankar Temple. Walk west to Jalebiwala, a century-old sweet shop, and then down Dariba Kalan Road for a spot of silver jewellery shopping. Then, head towards Meena Bazaar to the Jama Masjid, or go down Kinari Bazaar to delight in glittery wedding paraphernalia. Also stop by the Sunheri Masjid and, further down, Gurdwara Sisganj (see pp10–11).

### 6 Purani Dilli Havelis

Halfway down Chandni Chowk, on the right, is the well-preserved Chunna Mal Haveli. Walk up a few more blocks and take a left down Ballimaran to visit the famous Mirza Ghalib's house and then the Haveli Sharif Manzil. Double back towards Fatehpuri Masjid where in one of the alleys is Haveli Haider Quli, which displays many haveli architectural features.

Some haveli architectural features include arched gateways, carved doors, inner courtyard, high outer walls, and upper storey balcony.

### 7 Nizamuddin

The Nizamuddin Complex is best visited in the evening. There is much to occupy you – poet Mizra Ghalib's grave, delicious food at Dastarkhwan-e-Kareem, and just after the flower-sellers, the *dargahs* of Nizamuddin Aulia and Amir Khusrau *(see p90)*.

### 8 Purana Qila

The Purana Quila complex is quite compact, making it perfect for a lazy stroll. Start at the main gate, the Bara Darwaza and follow the paths that will lead you to the Qila-i-Kuhna Masjid, the Sher Mandal and several out-lying monuments *(see p89)*.

**Boats in the lake around the Purana Qila**

### 9 Northern Ridge

This often overlooked area is a treasure trove of forgotten monuments. Begin at the Ashokan pillar, opposite the main entrance of Hindu Rao Hospital. Further down the Ridge Road is the Mutiny Memorial. Then, go down Magazine Road to visit Flagstaff Tower *(see p84)*.

### 10 Around India Gate

The Mandi House area is a fantastic place to experience the cultural atmosphere of the city. Stop by the National School of Drama, Mandi House itself, Triveni Kala Sangam, Sahitya Academy and the Travancore Palace art gallery. ❂ *Map Q1* • *Mandi House, Copernicus Marg*

## Top 10 Outdoor Activities

### 1 Boating in Purana Qila

The lake adjacent to the Purana Qila has boats for hire. *Open daily summer: noon–7pm; winter: 11am–6pm*

### 2 Polo

Nothing like watching the steeds tear up the ground on a lazy afternoon. ❂ *Map M6* • *Race Course Road*

### 3 Ultimate Frisbee

Anyone can join in and play this sport. ❂ *Map L6* • *Nehru Park, Chanakyapuri* • *Every Sat noon*

### 4 Bird-watching

There are many bird-watching hot-spots in and around Delhi. ❂ *www.delhibird. netwww.delgigreens.com*

### 5 Rock Climbing

The Indian Mountaineering Foundation has several artificial walls for climbers. ❂ *6, Benito Juarez Road, Anand Niketan* • *2411 1211*

### 6 Picnic

For the less adventurous, Lodi Gardens is a perfect spot for a relaxing picnic. ❂ *Map N6*

### 7 Horse Riding

Go horse riding at the Delhi Riding Club. ❂ *Map M5* • *Safdarjung Road* • *2301 1891*

### 8 Cycling

The Delhi Cycling Club has everything from cycle polo to heritage cycle rides. ❂ *Map Q7* • *11/1, Jangpura Road, Bhogal* • *2437 3584*

### 9 Golfing

Hit the gorgeous greens of the Delhi Golf Club. ❂ *Map Q5* • *Dr Zakir Hussain Marg* • *2436 0002*

### 10 Swimming

Cool off at the lovely swimming pool at the Pacific Sports Complex. ❂ *Map W2* • *Greater Kailash 1* • *6565 0387*

Left **Traditional dolls, Dilli Haat** Centre **Shoppers at Hauz Khas Village** Right **Boxes, Sarojini Nagar**

# 🔟 Shops and Markets

**1 Chandni Chowk**
An area replete with the bustle of Old Delhi, here in Chandni Chowk you can find anything. There is silver jewellery at Dariba Kalan market, intricate *zardozi* embroidered saris at Kinari Bazaar, and textiles at Katra Neel market *(see pp10–11)*.

**2 State Emporia Complex**
This is a must-visit for anyone interested in India's crafts heritage. There is gold at the Andhra Pradesh emporium; beautiful saris at the Kerala emporium; *mojari* shoes, exquisite coir carpets and *dokra* art at The Rajiv Gandhi Handicrafts Bhavan; and lovely souvenirs at Tribes of India. ◈ *Map K4 • A 5, Baba Kharak Singh Marg • 2336 3081*

**3 Janpath**
A long colourful stretch of shops line the road that makes up this market. The rough-and-

**Curios and souvenirs at Janpath**

tumble stalls stock everything from export-reject clothes and traditional oils and perfumes to handmade paper lanterns and Tibetan knick-knacks and paintings. ◈ *Map F7 • Janpath Road • Open daily 10:30am–8pm*

**4 Khan Market**
Arguably the most chic spot in town, Khan Market boasts swanky shops and restaurants, including great bookstores such as Bahrisons and Full Circle, and home and decor shops such as Fabindia *(see p92)* and the gorgeous Good Earth *(see p92)*. There are smaller shops that sell lovely trinkets, handmade paper products and accessories ◈ *Map P5 • Open Mon–Sat 10am–7:30pm*

**5 Santushti**
This classy shopping complex is a pleasant place to browse for beautiful designer-wear and lifestyle products. There are lovely Kashmiri items at Lotus Eaters, while Ensemble brings together the country's top designers – such as Tarun Tahliani, Manish Arora and Rohit Bal – under one roof. ◈ *ITC Maurya Sheraton, Sardar Patel Marg • Open Mon–Sat 10am–7pm*

**6 Connaught Place**
The Georgian-style crescents of Connaught Place are a veritable treasure trove for shoppers. In Delhi's most important commercial space, brand showrooms rub shoulders with stores

*Curio shops near the gate to the ruins at Hauz Khas Village specialize in old Bollywood film posters – at bargain prices*

**Inner circle of Connaught Place**

established before Independence, offering a hectic spread of clothes, books and electronics. ✆ *Map F6 • Open Mon–Sat 9:30am–7pm*

### Hauz Khas Village
Woven around 13th-century Sultanate ruins, Hauz Khas Village has grown into a sophisti-cated shoppers' playground, although it still retains its quaint, rustic air. Its winding inner alleys throw up lovely surprises from art galleries and cafés to shops. ✆ *Map U2 • Hauz Khas Village • Open Mon–Sat 10am–7:30pm*

### Sarojini Nagar
Not for the faint-hearted, this chaotic maze of shops sells amazingly cheap heaps of export-reject clothes, among many other things, and is swamped by people. ✆ *Map V1 • Sarojini Nagar • Open Tue–Sun 10am–8:30pm*

### Dilli Haat
Built along the lines of a traditional Indian village market, Dilli Haat has a dizzying host of stores and stalls selling craft items from all over the country. ✆ *Map V1 • Opposite INA market • Open daily 10am–9pm • Adm*

### Select Citywalk Complex
This luxurious mall is home to many international brands as well as some home decor shops. Pop into PVR cinema for a movie, or visit the flea market on Wednesday evenings. ✆ *Map V3 • A 3, District Centre Saket • 4211 4211 • Open daily 10:30am–7:30pm*

## Top 10 Must-Buys

**1 Jewellery**
Pick up antique silver, contemporary platinum, beaded necklaces, or the eternal favourite, gold.

**2 Textiles**
Choose from an array of cotton, rich Benarasi silk, *khadi*, chiffon, crepe and more. Bespoke suits and outfits are also available at extremely reasonable prices.

**3 Craft Items**
India's rich crafts heritage is extremely well represented in Delhi. They are ideal for gifts and souvenirs.

**4 Home Decor**
Most stores stock products that are an exquisite blend of Indian and Western styles. Delicate work and traditional prints feature strongly.

**5 Clothes**
From export-reject items to exclusive designer wear Delhi has it all. Also popular are the many boutiques that stock unique pieces.

**6 Natural Cosmetics**
The trend for all things organic has given rise to some great indigenous brands such as Forest Essentials and Khadi.

**7 Tea**
The city is home to some of the world's best teas, includ-ing Darjeeling and Assam.

**8 Accessories**
Bags, shoes, belts and other accessories are available in a wide range of prices.

**9 Linen**
The fabrics found here are of excellent quality, with a focus on fine, traditional prints.

**10 Spices**
Take home some of the world's most aromatic spices, including saffron, cinnamon, pungent black pepper and fenugreek.

Left **Chef J. P. Singh at Bukhara, ITC Maurya Sheraton** Right **Threesixty Degrees at The Oberoi**

# Places to Eat

### Varq
Crimson beaded lamps, Mughal murals and mini *hawa mahals* jutting out from the walls. Varq couples these fancy flourishes with excellent Indian cuisine such as *varqui* crab, *martaban ka meat*, a delicious lamb curry, and irresistible *kulfi (see p77)*.

### Sagar Ratna
This vegetarian restaurant serves delicious South Indian cuisine, albeit in a slightly uninspired setting. The menu is well priced and authentic; try the *pesrat*, a lentil dosa stuffed with vermicelli and onion cooked in ghee, then wash it down with some tangy *rasam* (lentil soup) *(see p93)*.

### Olive Bar & Kitchen
Located in the rustic yet swanky One Style Mile, Olive Bar & Kitchen is one of the prettiest restaurants in town, with a lovely airy courtyard and the Qutb Minar providing a stunning backdrop. The food here, mainly Indian, Italian and Mediterranean, is delicious too, especially when paired with a wine from their extensive list *(see p99)*.

### The Lodhi
Perfect for a quiet, elegant occasion, The Lodhi specializes in Catalan cuisine accompanied by an impressive wine list and impeccable service. Starters are light: foie gras with pickled cherries; beetroot with Manchego and hazelnut. The mains are a treat, with amazing fish dishes, such as grilled tuna with chorizo and asparagus *(see p93)*.

### Bukhara
With a guest list that includes former US President Bill Clinton, Bukhara boasts a rich menu that includes the city's best-loved dishes. The buttery *dal bukhara* (lentils) is legendary, as is the melt-in-the-mouth lamb dish and *Sikandari raan (see p93)*.

### Wasabi
Dark wood sets the tone for this top-class Japanese restaurant. After a drink at the exclusive sake bar, sample steamed oysters followed by tenderloin *teppenyaki*. Round the meal off with a pungent yet surprisingly cooling wasabi sorbet *(see p77)*.

**Stylish interior of Wasabi**

**Plush interior of The Spice Route**

### The Spice Route
**7** This gorgeous venue is designed to reflect the art, culture and architecture along the Spice Route, from the Malabar Coast through Sri Lanka, Malaysia and Indonesia to Thailand and Vietnam. Be prepared for a culinary feast that draws on the cuisines of these regions *(see p77)*.

### Threesixty Degrees
**8** As its name might suggest, Threesixty Degrees brings together the best of world cuisine under one roof. There is a sushi station, a yakitori grill, an Indian tandoor and a wood-fire oven. The atmosphere here is young and vibrant *(see p93)*.

### The China Kitchen
**9** A far cry from the usual Indian-influenced Chinese fare served up in the city, the food in The China Kitchen is modern and experimental yet still deeply rooted in traditional, primarily Szechuan, flavours. Diners swear the Peking Duck is the best in Delhi *(see p99)*.

### Karim's
**10** Boasting a line of chefs that, apparently, used to prepare meals for Mughal emperors, Karim's is arguably the city's most famous culinary destination. Located in the bustle and chaos of Old Delhi, it serves legendary Mughlai fare including excellent mutton *korma* and stew, *seekh kebabs* and *bakrikhani (see p85)*.

## Top 10 Brunch Spots

**1 1911**
The 1911 serves excellent and varied Indian and continental in a lovely outdoor setting *(see p79)*.

**2 La Piazza**
La Piazza's all-you-can-eat Italian buffet includes some truly outstanding antipasti *(see p99)*.

**3 Kylin**
Salmon and asparagus rolls, among other pieces, are the highlights of Kylin's Sushi Sunday *(see p101)*.

**4 Punjabi By Nature**
A meat lover's heaven Punjabi by Nature, serves up endless meaty platters *(see p98)*.

**5 Oh! Calcutta**
A haven for authentic Bengali food, complete with old-world charm *(see p98)*.

**6 Sakura**
Delivers all-round excellence with *teppenyaki* and tempura counters, salads and sushi platters. ◉ *Map E7 • The Metropolitan Hotel, Bangla Sahib Road • 4250 0200 • Open Sun noon–3pm*

**7 Manré**
Alfresco lunch offering a Mongolian barbeque and continental grill *(see p99)*.

**8 Threesixty Degrees**
An extended world cuisine menu is on offer for brunch, along with free-flowing wine *(see p93)*.

**9 Lodi – The Garden Restaurant**
Lodi combines exquisite garden setting with fresh Mediterranean fare. ◉ *Map N6 • Lodi Road • 2465 2808 • Open noon–3:30pm*

**10 The China Kitchen**
There is a sumptous and wide-range of Chinese fare on offer at brunch *(see p99)*.

Left **Rattan loungers around the swimming pool at Aqua** Right **The stylish bar at Rick's**

# 🔟 Bars and Nightclubs

### Rick's
Inspired by the film *Casablanca*, this plush venue is considered one of the city's top bars and has much to recommend it – including some famous vodka-based cocktails and an endless wine list. The crowd is young, the atmosphere vibrant and the music ranges from cool jazz to retro 80s *(see p79)*.

### Aqua
This alfresco space is a visual treat, from the designer bar finished in aquamarine shades, to the iridescent pool. Make yourself comfortable on the rattan loungers in a curtained pavilion or, on one of the swings, while nibbling on the excellent Moroccan lamb cutlets *(see p79)*.

### 1911
Named for the year when the capital of the British Raj was shifted to New Delhi, 1911 is a quiet, elegant place steeped in old-world charm. The bar is all rich mahogany and Art Deco, while the lovely outdoor lounge overlooks the lawns *(see p79)*.

### Tapas Bar
This elegant basement-level bar at the Lodhi serves the most spectacular wine in town coupled with delectable treats. Try the *Jamon Iberico* (Iberian ham) and spicy chorizo or on a sunny afternoon, the fruity pomegranate sangria *(see p93)*.

### F Bar & Lounge
Join the glorious, glamorous people partying like there's no tomorrow at Delhi's poshest dance venue. The decor is a curious mix of Gothic chandeliers and colour-changing lights, which is easier on the eyes after a few deliciously lemony *ronellas* mai tais. 🅢 *Map L5 • The Ashok Hotel, 50 B, Diplomatic Enclave, Chanakyapuri • 2611 1066 • Open Sun–Thu 10:30am–4am; Fri–Sat 10:30am–5:30am*

**Ultraviolet lights at the bar in the F Bar & Lounge**

### Baci
A popular spot with the city's expatriate crowd, Baci is a refined option ideal for an early evening tête-à-tête. Come the weekend, and it transforms into a party hotspot. Apart from a long wine list, they serve superb and generous cocktails, especially the mojitos. All go well with their Italian finger food *(see p93)*.

*There is wine tasting at Tapas Bar every alternate Thursday evening.*

The extensive wine cellar at Enoteca

### Enoteca

The Enoteca bar is a warm little space that houses the Oberoi's 2,000-plus bottles of fine wine. Indulge in a bottle of Chateau Petrus Grand Vin, or something else from a list that includes wines from all arcoss the globe. ◈ Map R5 • The Oberoi, Dr Zakir Hussain Marg • 2436 3030 • Open daily 11am–midnight

### Polo Lounge

A smart bar with English-style leather and wood-panelling, a fireplace and old polo photographs and prints on the walls. Sink into a Chesterfield and muse over their comprehensive wine and spirits list (see p101).

### Kylin

Seek out this atmospheric bar, tucked away in a quiet corner of the bustling Priya Complex, and be rewarded with excellent cocktails, fruity sangria and superbly crisply Vietnamese spring rolls (see p101).

### ai, The Love Hotel

The Love Hotel's outdoors space is perfect for a pleasant Delhi winter evening. Sashay across the wooden walk-way and lounge around the long, stylish bar, while sipping a crisp green apple martini, or their exquisite peach martini (see p101).

## Top 10 Cocktails

**1 Wildberry Sour at The Yum Yum Tree**
A gigantic tumbler of chunky blackberries perfectly muddled with lime and vodka (see p99).

**2 Blushing Geisha at Kylin**
A delicate blend of heady sake, Malibu rum, melon liqueur and tart strawberry.

**3 Sangria at Tapas Bar**
Well-balanced sweetness, and full to the brim with fresh, crunchy fruit.

**4 Peach Martini at ai**
Fresh fruit and alcohol blended to perfection. Every visit to Delhi should involve trying this heavenly drink.

**5 Golden Martini at Magique**
A unique and perfectly satisfying blend of champagne and elderflower (see p99).

**6 Lychee Caipiroska at F Bar & Lounge**
Crisp and strong, without losing the flavour of the delicious fruit.

**7 Mojito at Stone**
A well-muddled mixture of brown sugar, lime and white rum. ◈ Map W1 • Moets Restaurant complex, Defence Colony Market • 6569 7689 • Open daily noon–midnight

**8 Cosmopolitan at Baci**
Delhi's best version of this classic: a tall, chilled glass that is not cloyingly sweet.

**9 Mud Slide at Shalom**
Dessert in a glass: vanilla ice cream, Kahlua and Baileys topped with Hershey's chocolate (see p101).

**10 Chocotini at Olive Beach**
A heady blend of coffee, Kahlua and a drizzle of Baileys. ◈ Map K4 • 9, Sardar Patel Marg, Chanakyapuri • 4604 0404 • Open daily noon–midnight

Left **The beautiful Alwar Fort** Right **Gardens laid out between pavilions at the Taj Mahal, Agra**

# Excursions from Delhi

## 1 Sultanpur Bird Sanctuary

Around 45 km (28 miles) west of Delhi in Haryana state, the Sultanpur Bird Sanctuary makes for a peaceful rural outing within fairly easy striking distance of Delhi. Centred on a large wetland area that fills up during the seasonal rains, the sanctuary attracts flocks of aquatic migratory birds and offers a number of lovely walks through the surrounding woods. ✆ Map B3 • Open daily sunrise–sunset • Adm and charge for video

**Religious poster in Mathura**

## 2 Mathura and Vrindavan

Mathura is reputed to be the be the birthplace of the flute-playing deity, Krishna, while half a million pilgrims a year flock to the nearby town of Vrindavan and the hill of Govardhan, which Krishna is said to have lifted with a single finger. ✆ Map C3

**Rich decoration in the Golden Temple, Amritsar**

## 3 Agra

Once capital of the entire Mughal Empire, the large and chaotic city of Agra is home to some of India's most inspiring monuments, including the impressive Agra Fort, the exquisite Itimad-ud-Daulah, Akbar's Tomb at Sikandra and, of course, the peerless Taj Mahal (see pp30–3).

## 4 Fatehpur Sikri

Around 40 km (25 miles) beyond Agra lie the fascinating remains of the ghost city of Fatehpur Sikri, built by Akbar between 1569 and 1585, but abandoned soon afterwards. The city remains wonderfully preserved, with superb red sandstone buildings and a magically time-warped atmosphere. ✆ Map C3 • Open daily sunrise–sunset • Adm

## 5 Amritsar

The holiest city of the Sikh faith is home to the world-famous Golden Temple, an unforgettable sight with its richly gilded central shrine, the Harmandir, rising serenely out of the surrounding lake. ✆ Map B1

## 6 Keoladeo Ghana National Park

This wonderful national park, near the town of Bharatpur is arguably India's finest bird-watching destination, home to a huge number of resident and migratory species including vast flocks of aquatic birds who come to nest around the park's extensive wetlands – adequate monsoon rainfall permitting. ◉ *Map C3 • Open Apr–Sep 6am–6pm; Oct–Mar 6:30am–5:30pm • Adm*

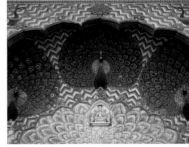

**Exquisite detail of a door in the City Palace, Jaipur**

### 7 Deeg

This workaday town is home to one of the region's most spectacular palaces. Built in the 18th century by the local Jat rulers, the Deeg Palace blends of Hindu and Mughal elements with spacious water gardens dotted with palaces and pavilions. The celebrated Kesav Bhavan (Monsoon Palace) was designed to recreate the torrential rainfall and thunderous sounds of a wet-season downpour. ◉ *Map B3 • Open daily 8am–5pm • Adm*

### 8 Alwar

Midway between Delhi and Jaipur, the characterful little city of Alwar is considered the traditional northern gateway to Rajasthan. It has an imposing fort with ramparts cresting a series of hills above the town, and an absorbing old city palace below. ◉ *Map B3*

### 9 Jaipur

Jaipur, the capital of Rajasthan, is a fascinating city with an abundance of attractions, ranging from the exuberant bazaars of the old Pink City to the regal City Palace and the Hawa Mahal, whose dramatic five-storey façade is one of India's most famous sights. ◉ *Map B3*

### 10 Sariska Tiger Reserve

An hour's drive past Alwar, the Sariska Tiger Reserve was at the centre of a huge controversy in 2005 when it was discovered that the park's entire tiger population had vanished, presumably taken by poachers. Even without the big cats the park is well worth a visit, however, with a wide range of birdlife and a good selection of Indian mammals ranging from jackals to antelopes. ◉ *Map B3 • Open daily: Jul–mid-Sep 8am–3pm; Apr–Jun & mid-Sep to Oct 6am–4pm; Nov–Mar 7am–3:30pm • Adm*

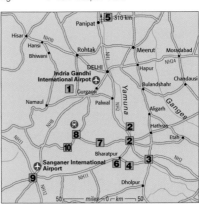

# AROUND TOWN

New Delhi
72–79

Old Delhi
80–85

South of the Centre
88–93

South Delhi
94–101

DELHI'S TOP 10

Left **Indira Gandhi Memorial Museum** Centre **Detail, Rashtrapati Bhavan gate** Right Shop in CP

# New Delhi

THE CITY OF NEW DELHI, *built by the British between 1911 and 1931, still serves as the hub of Delhi's increasingly huge and formless urban expanse. The area divides into two parts. The first is Connaught Place, at the commercial and residential heart of the city – a huge, vibrant circular plaza which is home to innumerable shops, restaurants and other businesses. The second, some 2 km (1 mile) south down Janpath, is the great Imperial thoroughfare of Rajpath, linking a triumphalist sequence of Raj-era landmarks, including India Gate and the Rashtrapati Bhavan. The area is also home to almost all the city's finest museums, plus a few relics dating back to the years before British rule.*

**National Museum sculpture**

## 🔟 Sights

1. Rajpath
2. Rashtrapati Bhavan
3. India Gate
4. National Museum
5. Crafts Museum
6. Indira Gandhi Memorial Museum
7. Gandhi Smriti Museum
8. Jantar Mantar
9. Connaught Place
10. Lakshmi Narayan Mandir

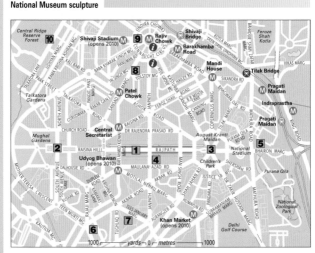

*New Delhi is well served by metro. Rajiv Chowk and Central Secretariat are the two most useful stations.*

### Rajpath

Originally named Kingsway, Rajpath is the ceremonial axis of Lutyens' New Delhi and links most of the major landmarks of the "new city". It runs all the way from India Gate via Vijay Chowk up Raisina Hill, between the two Secretariat Buildings and on to Rashtrapati Bhavan. The main section, between India Gate and Vijay Chowk, forms Delhi's most impressive open space: a huge boulevard flanked by lawns, with dramatic views of the Imperial monuments in all directions (see pp16–17).

The magnificent India Gate

### Rashtrapati Bhavan

The centrepiece of New Delhi is the Rashtrapati Bhavan; now the residence of the President of India, generally regarded as Lutyens' master-piece and India's finest example of Colonial-era architecture. The work is a remarkable synthesis of Neo-Classical and Indian styles, exemplified by the enormous dome said to have been model-led partly on the Pantheon in Rome and partly on the Buddhist stupa at Sanchi (see p17).

### India Gate

At the eastern end of Rajpath stands the imposing India Gate, built in 1921 to a design by Lutyens, who had experience of designing war memorials in Europe, including the famous Cenotaph on London's Whitehall. The monument was originally known as the All India War Memorial, built to commemorate the 90,000 soldiers of the British Indian Army killed during World War I and the Afghan Wars. The Tomb of the Unknown Soldier, or Amar Jawan Jyoti, was added in 1972 (see p16).

### National Museum

This is India's largest and most impressive museum with a vast collection of artifacts from prehistory to the 20th century. Highlights include a superb selection of ancient finds from the Harappan Civilization and an excellent collection of Indian miniatures, alongside huge quantities of Hindu and Buddhist sculpture. Also on display is an array of Chola bronzes including a famous statuette of the dancing Shiva (see pp26–9).

Entrance gate of the Rashtrapati Bhavan

Papier mâché products, Crafts Museum

### 5 Crafts Museum

Delhi's most entertaining and engaging museum offers an alternative take on the nation's cultural heritage. In contrast to the classic artworks at the National Museum, the emphasis here is on local artisanal traditions, showcasing an incredibly varied – and often quirky – range of cultural, religious and architectural traditions from across the subcontinent *(see pp22–3)*.

### 6 Indira Gandhi Memorial Museum

Formerly home to both Indira Gandhi and her son Rajiv, this moving museum was also the site of Indira's assassination (1984) by two of her Sikh bodyguards. There is a wide-ranging array of displays on Indira's years in power, offering a glimpse into both her achievements and lapses into quasi-dictatorship, plus an extensive collection of Rajiv's personal effects.

◈ Map M5 • 1, Safdarjung Road
• 2301 0094 • Open Tue–Sun 9:30am–4:45pm

### 7 Gandhi Smriti

It was here that Hindu fundamentalists assassinated Mahatma Gandhi in 1948. The museum serves simultaneously as an absorbing exposition of Gandhi's life and work and also as a shrine to one of the 20th-century's most inspirational leaders. Stone footsteps mark the route of Gandhi's last walk, while a small shrine in the garden marks the exact spot at which he was gunned down.

◈ Map N5 • 5, Tees January Marg
• 2301 1480 • Open Tue–Sun 10am–5pm
• http://gandhismriti.nic.in

### 8 Jantar Mantar

Jantar Mantar was one of five outdoor astronomical observatories constructed by the Maharaja of Jaipur, Jai Singh II (the others are in Jaipur, Mathura, Varanasi and Ujjain). Built in 1725, it consists of four huge, strangely-shaped stone instruments; these include the Samrat Yantra, a kind of monumental sundial centred on an enormous stone staircase, and the Misra Yantra, shaped like a huge inverted heart. The instruments were designed to perform various functions including measure precise solar and lunar calendars and the track the movements of stars and planets.

Gandhi statue in Gandhi Smriti

◈ Map F7 • Sansad Marg • Rajiv Chowk Metro • Open daily sunrise–sunset
• www.jantarmantar.org • Adm

### Connaught Place (CP)

The commercial hub of New Delhi, Connaught Place, or CP (now officially rechristened Rajiv Chowk), was built between 1929 and 1933 to a design by British architect Robert Tor Russell. The enormous circular plaza occupies a pivotal position in the layout of the new city, with roads radiating off in all directions. Built around a spacious central park, it is surrounded by colonnaded white Neo-Classical buildings, their shaded arcades hosting an excellent selection of upmarket shops and restaurants. ◈ Map F6
• Rajiv Chowk Metro

### Lakshmi Narayan Mandir

This huge wedding cake of a temple is the biggest and most striking of the various shrines along Mandir Marg, with a densely clustered mass of red and orange *shikharas* (towers) centred on a large marble courtyard. Shrines to Durga and a meditating Shiva stand within, while images of Ganesh and Hanuman can be found in the courtyard outside. ◈ Map D6
• Mandir Marg, near Connaught Place
• R. K. Ashram Marg Metro • Open daily 4:30am–noon & 2–9pm • No cameras or mobile phones allowed

Façade of Lakshmi Narayan Mandir

## A Day in New Delhi

### Morning

Begin your day exploring the varied exhibits at the engaging **Crafts Museum**, then walk along to the eastern end of **Rajpath** and **India Gate**. Continue on to the **National Museum** to spend a couple more hours browsing its superb array of Indian artifacts. Stop for lunch in the museum's pleasant top-floor restaurant, or alternatively take a rickshaw down to Khan Market, offering a wide variety of restaurants and cafes to choose from. Try **Café Turtle** (see p101) or **The Big Chill** or **Latitude** (see p93).

### Afternoon

Continue walking west along the stately expanse of Rajpath, as Herbert Baker's Neo-Classical **Secretariat Buildings** (see p76) come gradually into view. Carry on walking up to the top of Raisina Hill for a peek at Lutyens' masterpiece, **Rashtrapati Bhavan**; visits can be arranged by calling in advance (see p16). From here, catch a rickshaw, or walk via **Sansad Bhavan** (see p76), north to the unusual 18th-century outdoor astronomical park of **Jantar Mantar**. Take your time inspecting its intriguing planetary instruments, then walk another 100 metres north to **Connaught Place**, the heart of commercial New Delhi. Finish the day with a snack or a drink at one of the many restaurants, bars and cafés that this area has to offer, such as **1911**, **Triveni Tea Terrace**, **Q'Bar**, **Agni**, **Aqua**, **QashQai** or **Cha Bar** (see p79).

Left **Gurudwara Bangla Sahib** Right **Airy interior of the National Gallery of Modern Art**

# 🔟 Best of the Rest

### Ugrasen's Baoli
This spectacularly deep *baoli* (step well), now dry, is thought to have been built by Raja Agrasen (or Ugrasen) in the 15th century. ◈ *Map G7 • Off Hailey Road, Kasturba Gandhi Marg • Open daily*

### Hanuman Mandir
This temple boasts a richly decorated interior, brimful of religious atmosphere. ◈ *Map F7 • Baba Kharak Singh Marg • Open 5am–noon, 3pm–midnight*

### Gurudwara Bangla Sahib
The imposing Bangla Sahib is Delhi's most important Sikh *gurudwara* (temple). ◈ *Map E7 • Ashok Road • Open 24hrs*

### Jawaharlal Nehru Memorial Museum
The former home of India's first prime minister, with a series of period interiors preserved exactly as they were in Nehru's time. ◈ *Map L5 • Teen Murti Marg • 2341 4666 • Open Tue–Sun 10am–5pm*

### National Gallery of Modern Art (NGMA)
Housed in a superb modern building, with an outstanding range of Colonial and modern Indian art. ◈ *Map Q3 • Jaipur House • 2338 4640 • www.ngmaindia.gov.in*

### National Philatelic Museum
Philatelic paradise, with displays covering every stamp issued by India since Independence, as well as some older exhibits. ◈ *Map N2 • Dak Bhavan, Sardar Patel Chowk, Sansad Marg • 2303 6447 • Open Mon–Fri 10am–5pm*

### Secretariat Buildings
Herbert Baker's grandiose Secretariat Buildings, framing Raisina Hill, are two of the city's finest examples of epic Neo-Classical style. ◈ *Map M3 • Raisina Hill • Closed to the public*

### Sansad Bhavan
Designed by Edwin Lutyens, this huge circular edifice is home to the Indian parliament. ◈ *Map M2 • Lok Sabha Marg • Closed to the public*

### Cathedral Church of the Redemption
This quasi-Italianate structure is Delhi's grandest Anglican church and one of the city's last major Raj-era buildings (1935). ◈ *Map L2 • Church Road • Open daily*

### St Martin's Church
Built in 1930, this huge, fortress-like brick structure is one of Delhi's most unusual churches. ◈ *Map K4 • Off Cariappa Marg, near Dhaula Kuan and NH8*

For sight 3 see also **p52**; sights 4, 5, 6 see also **pp54–5**; sights 7, 8 and 9 see also **pp16–17**.

**Price Categories**
For a meal for one, inclusive of taxes and service charge but not alcohol.

| | |
|---|---|
| ® | under Rs.200 |
| ®® | Rs.200–500 |
| ®®® | Rs.500–750 |
| ®®®® | Rs.750–1,500 |
| ®®®®® | over Rs.1,500 |

Left **Sashimi platter at Wasabi** Right **Legends of India**

# 🔟 Places to Eat

### 1 Wasabi
This swanky restaurant serves excellent Japanese food. 🅂 *Map P4 • The Taj Mahal Hotel, 1, Man Singh Road • 2302 6162 • Open daily 12:30–2:30pm; 7–11:30pm • ®®®®®*

### 2 Varq
A stylish, relaxed place that serves some truly delicious Indian food. Try lamb cooked in a saffron crust or crispy Calicut prawns. 🅂 *Map P4 • The Taj Mahal Hotel, 1, Man Singh Road • 2302 6162 • Open daily 2:30–2:45pm; 7:30–11:45pm • ®®®®®*

### 3 The Spice Route
A combination of gorgeous decor and fine cuisine inspired by the culture of places along the Spice Route. 🅂 *Map F7 • The Imperial, 1, Janpath Road • 2334 1234 • Open daily 12:30–3pm; 7:30–11:30pm • ®®®®®*

### 4 Veda
An opulent restaurant that serves top-notch food – from the *murgh malai tikka* to delicious Parsi sea bass. 🅂 *Map F6 • H 27, Connaught Place • 4151 3535 • Open daily noon–2:30 pm, 6–11:30pm • ®®®®®*

### 5 Saravana Bhavan
An institution when it comes to authentic South Indian food. Try the mini-tiffin. 🅂 *Map F6 • P 15, Connaught Place, Outer Circle • 2331 6060 • Open daily 8am–11pm • ®*

### 6 Rajdhani
Serving up almost-authentic Gujarati food, this no-frills place is perfect for a quick vegetarian thali. 🅂 *Map F6 • P 90, Daulatram House, Connaught Place • 2334 6300 • Open daily noon–3:30pm; 7–11pm • ®*

### 7 Legends of India
A quiet space in the bustle of Connaught Place, this serves fairly decent Indian food. 🅂 *Map F6 • N 56, Connaught Place • 4301 2322 • Open daily 12:30–11:45pm • ®®®®*

### 8 19 Oriental Avenue
Stylish and slick, serving simple Japanese food with a smattering of Thai and Chinese. 🅂 *Map E7 • 19, Ashoka Road, Connaught Place • 4119 1919 • Open daily noon–2:45pm; 7–11:45pm • ®®®®®*

### 9 Mosaic
At Mosaic, you can travel the culinary breadth of India. 🅂 *Map F6 • M 45/1, Connaught Place • 2341 6842 • Open daily noon–4pm; 6pm–midnight • ®®*

### 10 Daniell's Tavern
A lovely place inspired by the travels of the late 18th-century artists Thomas and William Daniell. 🅂 *Map F7 • The Imperial, 1, Janpath Road • 2334 1234 • Open daily 12:30–2:45pm; 7–11:45pm • ®®®®*

Left **The Shop, Connaught Place** Right **Hand-crafted dolls at the Crafts Museum**

# 🔟 Places to Shop

### 1 The Shop
The Shop is an excellent stop for beautiful ethnic Indian home and lifestyle products. ✎ *Map F6*
• *10, Regal Building, Connaught Place*
• *2334 0971 • Open Mon–Sat*

### 2 People Tree
Imaginative and colourful apparel created by a group of artists and designers committed to social and environmental causes. ✎ *Map F6 • 8, Regal Building, Parliament Road, Connaught Place • 2374 4877 • Open Mon–Sat*

### 3 Central Cottage Industries Emporium
A government initiative set up to preserve and develop handicrafts from all over the country. ✎ *Map F7 • Jawahar Vyapar Bhavan, Janpath • 2332 0439 • Open Mon–Sat*

### 4 Khadi
Another government initiative supporting the production of Indian fabrics, natural cosmetics, organic food, pottery products and handmade paper. ✎ *Map F6*
• *Khadi Gramodyog Bhavan, 24, Regal Building, Connnaught Place*
• *2341 6514 • Open daily*

### 5 Tribes of India
A store that stocks lovely tribal handicrafts from all over the country. ✎ *Map F7 • Gallery 2, Rajiv Gandhi Handicrafts Bhavan, Baba Kharag Singh Marg • 2334 1282 • Open Mon–Sat*

### 6 Industree
Industree stocks a splendid array of home accessories crafted from natural fibre, and eco-friendly furniture. ✎ *Map F7 • Gallery 8, Rajiv Gandhi Handicrafts Bhavan, Baba Kharag Singh Marg • 2336 8395 • Open Mon–Sat*

### 7 Kamala
Kamala offers exotic jewellery, toys, folk paintings, pottery, bric-a-brac and hand-woven and printed fabrics.
✎ *Map F7 • Gallery 1, Rajiv Gandhi Handicrafts Bhavan, Baba Kharag Singh Marg • 6596 6900 • Open Mon–Sat*

### 8 Girdhari Lal
Famous for its exquisite handmade jewellery, Girdhari Lal offers stone pendants, hand-beaten bangles and delicate earrings. ✎ *Map F6 • 9 N, Connaught Place • 2331 6479 • Open Mon–Sat*

### 9 Crafts Museum Shop
Housed within the excellent Crafts Museum *(see pp22–3)*, this shop stocks exquisite folk art items and home decor products in ethnic designs.

### 🔟 Tibetan Curios
Lining the walls of this little shop are *thankhas* (devotional paintings), traditional Tibetan wear, prayer bells and pretty jewellery.
✎ *Map F7 • 14, Tibetan Market, Janpath • 2336 8691 • Open Mon–Sat*

Left **The pool at Aqua** Right **The neon-lit bar at Agni, The Park**

# 🔟 Bars and Cafés

### 1 Rick's
Everyone's favourite bar in town, Rick's is understated and intimate, and has an extensive wine list. 🟤 *Map P4 • The Taj Mahal Hotel, 1, Man Singh Road • 2302 6162 • Open daily 12:30pm–12:30am*

### 2 Aqua
A glamorous alfresco space complete with a sparkling pool, pretty white curtained pavilions and swing-seats. 🟤 *Map F7 • The Park, 15, Parliament Street • 2374 3000 • Open daily 7–11:45pm*

### 3 1911
The 1911 is replete with old-world charm, best enjoyed on a sunny afternoon over a chilled beer, in the seating area that overlooks the hotel lawns. 🟤 *Map F7 • The Imperial, 1, Janpath Road • 2334 1234 • Open daily 4:30pm–midnight*

### 4 Triveni Tea Terrace
Sharing space with four art galleries, this is a charming spot to relax in after browsing an exhibition. 🟤 *Map Q1 • Triveni Kala Sangam, Tansen Marg • 2371 8833 • Open Mon–Sat 10am–7pm*

### 5 Cha Bar
Housed in the Oxford Bookstore, the Cha Bar boasts an extensive tea list and is a great place to unwind. 🟤 *Map G7 • 148, Barakhamba Road, Statesman House, Connaught Place • 2376 6083 • Open Mon–Sat 9am–6pm*

### 6 Qashqai
This understated lounge bar is ideal for a quiet cocktail or two. 🟤 *Map F6 • M 89/90, Connaught Place • 4350 7880 • Open daily 7pm–1am*

### 7 Q'Bar
Sit out on the gorgeous terrace complete with pretty umbrellas, fairy lights, lovely wrought-iron furniture and a great view of Connaught Place. 🟤 *Map F6 • E 42/43, Connaught Place • 4151 2888 • Open daily noon–midnight*

### 8 Agni
Loud and fun, Agni is the place to be if you are in the mood for *bhangra* (Punjabi dance). 🟤 *Map F7 • The Park, Parliament Street, Connaught Place • 2374 3000 • Open daily 11am–1am*

### 9 Legends of India Tea Terrace
Reminiscent of an old-fashioned gentlemen's club, this is a charming spot for afternoon tea, or a beer. 🟤 *Map F6 • N 56, Connaught Place, Outer Circle • 4301 2322 • Open daily 12:30–11:45pm*

### 10 Sam's Cafe
Located on a high terrace above the Paharganj bazaar, Sam's Café is the perfect place to unwind and listen to some Tibetan rock music. 🟤 *Map E5 • 1534–50 Main Bazaar, Paharganj • 4154 1436 • Open daily 9am–10pm*

Left **Aerial view of the Jama Masjid** Right *Biryani* **stall near the Jama Masjid**

# Old Delhi

THE CITY OF SHAHJAHANABAD, *originally built by Mughal Emperor Shah Jahan between 1638 to 1648 to replace the previous Mughal capital of Agra (see pp32–3) and now generally known as Old Delhi, is without a doubt the most rewarding and intriguing part of the city. This is Delhi at its most traditional and atmospheric: a fascinating labyrinth honeycombed with tiny alleyways and numerous colourful bazaars and dotted with a seemingly endless profusion of historical monuments and religious shrines including two of Delhi's landmark attractions: the magnificent Mughal-era Red Fort and the grand Jama Masjid. There are further – albeit more modest – points of interest north of Old Delhi itself in the quiet Civil Lines district, where the British first established themselves in the city, and along the lush Northern Ridge, where they sought refuge during the opening months of the 1857 Uprising.*

**Shops in Chandni Chowk**

## 🔟 Sights

1. Red Fort
2. Jama Masjid
3. Chandni Chowk
4. Raj Ghat
5. Bazaars of Old Delhi
6. Zinat ul Masjid
7. St James' Church
8. Tomb of Razia Sultan
9. Ajmeri Gate
10. Lal Mandir

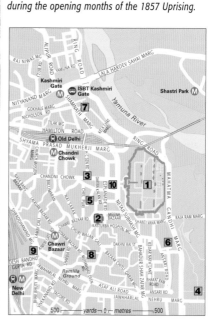

*A good map or street atlas (see p106) is essential for navigating the disorienting labyrinth of Old Delhi's backstreets.*

**Delicate filigree marble screen of the Khas Mahal, Red Fort**

### Red Fort
The enormous Red Fort served as the residence of the Mughal emperors from its completion in 1648 through to the 1857 Uprising, when the last emperor, Bahadur Shah Zafar II, was exiled to Burma and the British took over the fort, demolishing many of its buildings. What is left now is only a shadow of the original complex, but the surviving pavilions and gardens still give a sense of the sophisticated lifestyles of India's most powerful and cultured rulers *(see pp8–9)*.

**Turmeric in Chandni Chowk**

### Jama Masjid
The Jama Masjid is unquestionably the most beautiful of Old Delhi's Mughal monuments, looming high above the surrounding streets on a natural hillock and dominating all views of the old city. The approach from Meena Bazaar up to the eastern gate, facing the Red Fort, is particularly dramatic, although visitors now have to enter via the rather less imposing gateway on the western side *(see pp12–13)*.

### Chandni Chowk
Old Delhi's main thoroughfare, and one of the most colourful streets in the city, Chandni Chowk runs dead straight from the gates of the Red Fort due west to the Fatehpuri Masjid *(see p11)*, passing an eclectic range of shops and shrines en route. The road's name, meaning Moonlit Square, is said to refer to a square that once stood about halfway along the road, and which was known for the moonlit reflections in the canal that ran through its centre *(see pp10–11)*.

### Raj Ghat
These spacious gardens, set back from the banks of the Yamuna River, are best known as the place where the funeral rites of many of modern India's most important leaders were performed. Most notable among these is perhaps Gandhi, who was cremated here in 1948, and whose simple marble memorial still draws large crowds of reverent visitors. Other memorials dot the lawns, marking the places where the funeral sites of other national leaders, including Shanti Vana (Jawaharlal Nehru), Shakti Sthal (Indira Gandhi) and Vir Bhumi (Rajiv Gandhi).
*Map J5 • Mahatma Gandhi Marg • Open daily Apr–Sep 5am–7:30pm, Oct–Mar 5:30am–7pm*

### Bazaars of Old Delhi

**5** Although much of the physical fabric of Old Delhi is fairly modern – the result of damage sustained during the 1857 Uprising and 20th-century rebuilding – the entire area retains its original, labyrinthine street plan and much of its traditional atmosphere. Different areas are devoted to different trades and crafts – from jewellery and wedding gifts to fireworks and spare car parts – with thousands of shoebox shops tucked away amidst a confusion of narrow, twisting streets *(see pp46–7).*

### Zinat ul Masjid

**6** Hidden away in the streets of Daryaganj, this lovely mosque was commissioned in 1707 by Aurangzeb's daughter, Zinat ul Nisa, and is popularly known as the Ghata Masjid. Zinat ul Nisa was buried here following her death in 1711, but her tomb was apparently removed by the British after the uprising, when the mosque was taken over for military use. **✪** *Map J4 • Ghata Masjid Road, Daryaganj • Taxi or rickshaw • Open daily sunrise–sunset*

**Façade and striped domes of Zinat ul Masjid**

### St James' Church

**7** This little Neo-Classical gem was built by Colonel James Skinner in 1836 – a perfect period piece, constructed in an unusual cruciform pattern with a large dome over the central crossing. Memorials to some of the city's

**The Neo-Classical St James' Church**

most colourful early British residents stand in and around the church, including William Fraser, Thomas Metcalfe *(see p21)* and Skinner himself. **✪** *Map G2 • Sham Nath Marg • Kashmiri Gate Metro • Open daily 9am–1pm & 2–5pm*

### Tomb of Razia Sultan

**8** The tomb of Razia Sultan occupies an atmospheric little roofless enclosure deep in the heart of the old city. It was built here, long before the city that now surrounds it, for its proximity to the tomb of Sufi saint Shah Turkman (d.1240), of whom Razia was a devoted follower. The second tomb on the central platform is thought to be that of Razia's sister. **✪** *Map G5 • Off Sitaram Bazaar Road • Chawri Bazaar Metro • Open sunrise–sunset*

---

#### Razia Sultan: Queen of India

The indomitable Razia Sultan (r.1236–40) was the subcontinent's only woman ruler before Indira Gandhi. Razia broke every sexual stereotype of her macho and militaristic age: dressing as a man, leading her troops into battle and proving to be a competent ruler. Inspite of her efforts, she was overthrown and killed after four years on the throne.

### Ajmeri Gate

Marooned on a small island amidst busy traffic, this is perhaps the most impressive of the four surviving gateways that once punctuated the old city walls. The fine old *madrasa* and Mosque of Ghazi-ud-Din, built in classic Mughal style, stand just opposite. Elsewhere in the old city, the Delhi, Kashmiri and Turkman gates also survive in good condition – the last is named after the revered Sufi saint, Hazrat Shah Turkman, who is buried nearby. ⊗ *Map G4 • Ajmeri Gate Road • Chawri Bazaar Metro*

### Lal Mandir

Delhi's most important Jain temple, Lal Mandir is located directly opposite the Red Fort, at the southern end of Chandni Chowk. Founded under Shah Jahan for the Jain soldiers in his army, the present building dates from the 1870s. The colourful interior is adorned with dozens of diminutive statues of various Jain *tirthankaras*. The temple's well-known bird hospital stands next door, caring for hundreds of hungry and injured pigeons and other feathered creatures, packed into tiny cages *(see p10)*.

**Distinctive red domes of Lal Mandir**

## A Day in Old Delhi

### Morning

Start your day at the **Red Fort** – arrive early, if you can, to avoid the crowds. Spend a couple of hours exploring the complex; the pleasant Dawat Khana café at its far end is a good spot for a coffee. Exit the fort and walk up **Chandni Chowk**, stopping by some or all of the various attractions en route. Stop at **Haldiram's** *(see p85)*, halfway up the road, for a tasty Indian fast-food lunch, then, for dessert, hop across the road to the famous **Ghantewala's** *(see p11)* to sample some of their legendary sweets.

### Afternoon

Carry on up Chandni Chowk to the **Fatehpuri Masjid** *(see p11)*, then on to the remarkable spice market of Khari Baoli, just beyond. From here, you can either retrace your steps down Chandni Chowk, then turn, right down Dariba Kalan, or alternatively head down Ballimaran to visit the great Urdu poet's – Mirza Ghalib – haveli and then **Chawri Bazaar**, through the heart of Old Delhi's bazaars. Much of the fun here lies in simply wandering at will; aim to get lost at least once. Whichever route you take, try to be at the **Jama Masjid** towards sunset, when this superb mosque is at its most memorable, and the views over the old city and Red Fort are at their best. On leaving the Jama Masjid, you will find you are within a few steps of one of Old Delhi's culinary institutions, **Karim's** *(see p85)*, the perfect spot for an early dinner.

Left **Mirza Ghalib Haveli** Right **Stone structures in Qudsia Bagh**

# Best of the Rest

### 1 Mirza Ghalib Haveli
The former home of the great Urdu poet Mirza Ghalib (1797–1869) is now carefully restored and reopened as a simple little museum with a few modest exhibits on the writer's life and times. ⊗ *Map G3 • Qasimjan Street, off Ballimaran • Open Tue–Sun 10am–5pm*

### 2 Feroz Shah Kotla
All that remains of Sultan Feroz Shah Tughlaq's erstwhile citadel – now popularly thought to be the abode of djinns (spirits). ⊗ *Map J6 • Bahadur Shah Zafar Marg • Open daily sunrise–sunset • Adm*

### 3 Gauri Shankar Temple
One of Old Delhi's largest and most popular Hindu temples *(see p10)*, dedicated to god Shiva (Shankar) and his consort Parvati (Gauri). ⊗ *Map H3 • Chandni Chowk*

### 4 Nicholson's Cemetery
This beautiful Colonial-era cemetery contains the grave of Brigadier-General John Nicholson, who led (and was killed in) the British assault on Delhi during the 1857 Uprising. ⊗ *Map G1 • Lala Hardev Sahai Marg • Open daily*

### 5 Qudsia Bagh
Peaceful wooded gardens just north of the old city, home to a couple of fine buildings dating back to the garden's foundation during the 18th-century. ⊗ *Map G1 • Lala Hardev Sahai Marg • Open daily sunrise–sunset*

### 6 Northern Ridge
Rising up north of Old Delhi, this long, wooded ridge saw fierce fighting during the uprising, but is now one of the most peaceful spots in town, dotted with Tughlaq and British monuments. ⊗ *Map E1*

### 7 Ashoka Column
At the southern end of the Nothern Ridge is one of the city's two Ashokan columns, dating from the reign of Ashoka (r.269–232 BC), brought from Meerut in the 14th century by Feroz Shah Tughlaq. ⊗ *Map E1 • Rani Jhansi Road • Open daily*

### 8 Chauburji Masjid
A Tughlaq-era ruins in the Northern Ridge, this structure was built as a tomb around 1345, and subsequently converted into a mosque. ⊗ *Map B4 • Magazine Road • Open daily sunrise–sunset*

### 9 Pir Ghaib
These crumbling remains are all that survives of a palatial hunting lodge built here by Feroz Shah Tughlaq in the 14th century. ⊗ *Map F1 • Ridge Road • Open daily*

### 10 National Gandhi Museum
At the southern end of the expansive Raj Ghat gardens, this engaging little museum offers endearingly personal insights into the Mahatma's remarkable life and works. ⊗ *Map J5 • Raj Ghat • 2331 1793 • Open Tue–Sat, every other Sun 9:30am–5:30pm*

**Price Categories**

For a meal for one, inclusive of taxes and service charge but not alcohol.

| | |
|---|---|
| ® | under Rs.200 |
| ®® | Rs.200–500 |
| ®®® | Rs.500–750 |
| ®®®® | Rs.750–1,500 |
| ®®®®® | over Rs.1,500 |

Buffet amidst the eclectic furnishings at Chor Bizarre

# 🔟 Places to Eat

### 1 Karim's

This Delhi institution has been doling out delicious Mughlai food for over half a century. ® Map H4 • 16, Gali Kababiyan, Matia Mahal, Jama Masjid • 2326 9880 • Open daily 7am–midnight • ®®

### 2 Chor Bizarre

One of the oldest restaurants in Old Delhi, Chor Bizarre is famous for its superb Kashmiri cuisine. ® Map H5 • Hotel Broadway, 4/15A, Asaf Ali Road • 2327 3840 • Open daily 12:30–3:30pm; 7:30–11:30pm • ®®®®

### 3 Paranthe-wali Gully

The "alley of parantha-makers" is a foodie's delight, offering an overwhelming variety of this stuffed Indian bread. ® Map G3 • Opposite Natraj Restaurant, 1396, Chandni Chowk • Open daily • ®

### 4 Haldiram's

This place specializes in good Indian street food and sweets prepared in hygienic conditions. ® Map G3 • 1454/2, Chandni Chowk • 2883 3007 • Open daily 9am–11pm • ®

### 5 Moti Mahal

Dating back to Independence, this restaurant reputedly invented the famous butter chicken. ® Map H5 • 3704 Netaji Subhash Marg, Daryaganj • 2327 3011 • Open daily 11am–midnight • ®®

### 6 Embassy Restaurant

An old-world restaurant reminiscent of Colonial clubs, serving standard North Indian fare. ® Map G1 • 13, Alipur Road, Civil Lines • 2399 3061 • Open daily noon–3:30pm; 7:30pm–12:30am • ®®®®

### 7 The Curzon Room

Dig into the sumptuous lunch buffet at this airy, elegant Raj-style restaurant. ® Map G1 • Oberoi Maidens, 7, Sham Nath Marg, Civil Lines • 2397 5464 • Open daily 1–3pm; 7:30–11pm • ®®®®®

### 8 The Garden Terrace

Spilling into a lovely courtyard, this is an ideal place for nursing a cup of coffee. ® Map G1 • Oberoi Maidens, 7, Sham Nath Marg, Civil Lines • 2397 5464 • Open daily 7am–11pm • ®®®®

### 9 Gujarati Samaj

A family-run, canteen-style restaurant that serves fuss-free Gujarati food. ® Map F1 • 2, Raj Niwas Marg, Civil Lines • 2398 1796 • Open daily 10am–10:30pm • ®

### 10 Kake di Hatti

This nondescript-looking joint has drawn flocks of locals since 1965 to mop up its legendary *daal makhni*. ® Map G3 • 654, Church Mission Road, Fatehpuri, Chandni Chowk • 98109 09754 • Open daily 7:30am–12:30pm • ®

Left **Shop in Nizamuddin** Centre **Water lilies in Lodi Gardens** Right **Rhino in Delhi Zoo**

# South of the Centre

THE AREA IMMEDIATELY SOUTH OF NEW DELHI *is now home to some of the city's most upmarket suburbs, with an enticing range of stylish restaurants and boutique shops, although attractions for the visitor are mainly historical, with a superb swathe of Mughal (and some Sultanate) monuments built during an era when this part of the city was still largely untouched countryside. Top of most visitors' lists is the magnificent Humayun's Tomb, the first great masterpiece of Mughal architecture, though there are also stand-out attractions nearby at the wonderfully atmospheric religious enclave of Nizamuddin, the beautiful parklands and historic monu-*

*ments of the Lodi Gardens, the chintzy Safdarjung's Tomb, and the rugged citadel of Purana Qila, while just across the Yamuna River lies the astonishingly flamboyant Akshardham Temple, India's most extravagant modern Hindu shrine.*

**Humayun's Tomb**

## 🔟 Sights

| | | | |
|---|---|---|---|
| 1 | Humayun's Tomb | 6 | Safdarjung's Tomb |
| 2 | Delhi Zoo | 7 | Nizamuddin |
| 3 | Akshardham Temple | 8 | Lodi Gardens |
| 4 | Purana Qila | 9 | Khan-i-Khanan's Tomb |
| 5 | Khair ul Manazil Masjid | 10 | National Rail Museum |

### Humayun's Tomb

One of the greatest of all Mughal garden tombs, this superb mausoleum is one of Delhi's finest monuments and a magnificent memorial to the personable but erratic Humayun, the second Mughal emperor. The tomb established all the major hallmarks of the

**Screen of the Barber's Tomb, Humayun's Tomb Complex**

Mughal style, which was to reach its final apotheosis in the Taj Mahal: epic in scale, but simple in effect (see pp14–15).

### Delhi Zoo

The largest in India, Delhi's popular zoo is home to around 2,000 animals, including national treasures such as rhinos, elephants and Bengal tigers, and a good selection of wildlife from the Americas, Australia and Africa. Spread out over expansive parkland, it provides a sympathetic environment for its captive animals, as well as a pleasant refuge for the city's human population. It is also a great spot for a picnic. ◈ Map R4 • Mathura Road, near Purana Qila • Pragati Maidan Metro • Open summer 8am–6pm; winter 9am–5pm; Closed Fri • Adm • http://delhizoo.wordpress.com

### Akshardham Temple

Opened in 2005, this is perhaps the largest and most spectacular modern Hindu temple in India. The huge complex is centred on an extravagant central shrine, ringed by 148 elephant statues; inside is a huge golden figure of Bhagwan Shri Swaminarayan, in whose honour the temple was built. ◈ Map C5 • Taxi or Akshardham Metro • Open Tue–Sat Apr–Sep 10am–7pm; Oct–Mar 9am–6pm
• Electronic equipment not allowed
• www.akshardham.com

### Purana Qila

The sixth "city" of Delhi, the Purana Qila was begun by Humayun and completed by his rival Sher Shah Suri. Its large and rugged walls stretch for over a mile and enclose a large swathe of parkland, dotted with various buildings. The two most notable are the imposing Qala-i-Kuhna Masjid, and the more delicate Sher Mandal, an unusual little octagonal pavilion which was used by Humayun as a library and observatory. ◈ Map R3
• Mathura Road • Pragati Maidan Metro
• Open daily sunrise–sunset • Adm

**The formidable walls and gate of the Purana Qila**

Around Town – South of the Centre

### 5 Khair ul Manazil Masjid

Just across the road from the Purana Qila lies the impressive, though now rather derelict, Khair ul-Manazil Masjid, built in 1562 by Maham Angah, the powerful wet-nurse of Akbar. The mosque is a classic example of early Mughal architecture, its low and rather stocky façade reminiscent of the earlier Sultanate style. ✆ *Map Q4 • Mathura Road, opposite Purana Qila • Pragati Maidan Metro • Open sunrise–sunset*

Gilded wall with Islamic inscriptions, Nizamuddin *dargah*

### 6 Safdarjung's Tomb

This well-known mausoleum was built in 1754 for Safdarjung (1708–54), the Nawab of Awadh and one of the most important Mughal nobles during the reigns of Muhammad Shah and Ahmad Shah Bahadur whom he served briefly as *wazir* (chief minister). A good example of late-Mughal design, the tomb is a large and floridly decorated sandstone structure with a bulbous dome set in a *charbagh*-style garden. ✆ *Map M6 • Aurobindo Road • Taxi, auto-rickshaw or Race Course Metro • Open daily sunrise–sunset • Adm*

The flamboyant façade of Safdarjung's Tomb

### 7 Nizamuddin

This atmospheric religious enclave grew up around the tomb of the great Sufi saint Sheikh Nizamuddin Aulia (1236–1325), and remains busy with pilgrims at all hours, with performances of devotional *qawaali* singing after dark. It is also home to a cluster of Mughal monuments and the graves of various notable individuals, including the poet and musician Amir Khusrau (1253–1325), Shah Jahan's daughter Princess Jahanara and the great 19th-century Urdu poet Mirza Ghalib (see p84). ✆ *Map R6 • Hazrat Nizamuddin Station • Open 24 hrs*

### 8 Lodi Gardens

The beautiful Lodi Gardens is one of Delhi's most attractive retreats, offering a beguiling combination of nature and culture, with idyllic wooded landscape dotted with a sequence of fine tombs dating from the Lodi and Sayyid dynasties (see pp24–5).

### 9 Khan-i-Khanan's Tomb

This grandiose tomb is the burial place of Abdur Rahim, Akbar's prime minister, who died in 1626, although it may have been built for his wife, who passed away in 1598. The tomb has four grand *iwans* and a bulbous central dome surrounded by *chattris*, rather like a sketch for the Taj Mahal (minus the

A dargah *is a Muslim shrine for a saint.*

## Last Rites, Delhi-style

No other city in the world boasts as copious an array of mausoleums as Delhi – from certain angles the city can look like a kind of enormous necropolis. Oddly enough, such buildings run directly contrary to Koranic orthodoxy, which forbids the construction of elaborate funerary monuments – a prohibition that was ignored by the city's rulers.

minarets). Most of the sandstone facing on its walls was removed (it is said) for use in Safdarjung's Tomb. ◈ *Map R7 • Mathura Road, south of Humayun's Tomb • Open daily sunrise–sunset • Adm*

**Mono-Rail, National Rail Museum**

### 10 National Rail Museum

The National Rail Museum is a shrine to India's fascination with all things pertaining to the train. Among the highlights are the lavish carriages created for local and foreign aristocrats, ranging from the Maharaja of Mysore to the Prince of Wales. There is also a selection of antique steam engines as well as models, mannequins, photographs and other locomotive exhibits. ◈ *Map U1 • Satya Marg, Chanakyapuri • 2616 1816 • Open Tue–Sun: Apr–Sep 9:30am–1pm & 1:30–7pm, Oct–Mar 9:30am–1pm & 1:30–5pm • www.nationalrailmuseum.org • Adm and charge for video*

## A Day in the South of the Centre

### Morning

🕐 It is possible to see most of the major sights covered in this section in one long, albeit very busy, day. Note that you will need to pick up auto-rickshaws to get between them, or hire a taxi or auto-rickshaw for the day. The highlights of the **Akshardham Temple** can be seen in two hours, but for a more leisurely visit, allow half a day. Alternatively, you could pick from the following selection for a more relaxed tour.

Start your day at the brooding **Purana Qila**, then cross the road to visit the **Khair ul-Manazil Masjid**. From here, you can walk (or catch an auto-rickshaw) south to Sundar Nagar Market for an early lunch at **Baci** *(see p93)*. Then, catch another auto-rickshaw to **Humayun's Tomb**.

### Afternoon

Explore Humayun's Tomb and the other mausoleums that dot the vast complex, then walk across the road to the wonderful little *dargah* at **Nizamuddin**. Catch another auto-rickshaw down Lodi Road to **Lodi Gardens**. Stroll around the gardens at leisure, exploring the various tombs that dot the beautiful parkland – don't miss the Bonsai garden. Walk a short distance down the road to the imposing **Safdarjung's Tomb**. Then catch an auto-rickshaw to the nearby Santushti complex and end your day with a drink or an early dinner at **Basil and Thyme** *(see p93)*.

Left **Earings at Amrapali** Centre **Bag at Ogaan Closet** Right **The Bookshop**

# Places to Shop

### Fabindia
Fabindia is popular for printed cotton clothes, but it also stocks furniture, linen, organic foods and cosmetics. ✎ Map P5
• Central Hall, Khan Market • 4368 3100

### Anokhi
Specializing in contemporary crafted textiles with their roots in Jaipur, Anokhi stocks beautiful ethnic and western wear. ✎ Map P5 • 32, Khan Market • 2460 3423

### Good Earth
This luxurious store stocks exclusively designed dining products, high-quality linen and lovely home decor items. ✎ Map P5 • 9 ABC, Khan Market • 2464 7175

### Mittal Tea House
Stuffed floor to ceiling with speciality products, Mittal Tea House stocks beautifully packed Darjeeling, Assam and Nilgiri teas as well as Kangra and Kashmiri green teas. ✎ Map P7 • 8 A, Lodi Colony Market • 2461 5709

### Silverline
The walls of this busy shop are lined with beautiful jewellery in antique, ethnic and contemporary designs. ✎ Map P5 • 7 A, Khan Market • 2464 3017

### Amrapali
The exclusive collection here includes exquisite contemporary jewellery, designer, enamel, ethnic and antique pieces. ✎ Map P5 • 39, Khan Market • 4175 2024

### Ogaan Closet
This shop has a splendid ensemble of clothes, accessories and jewellery by various Indian designers. It provides a platform for Indian design and stocks luxurious clothes that are exquisite in cut and design. ✎ Map P5 • 77, Khan Market • 4175 7301

### The Bookshop
Tucked away in a quiet corner of the Jor Bagh market, The Bookshop is lovingly stocked with a wide range of reading matter, from well-thumbed classics to pristine new arrivals. ✎ Map N7 • 13/7, Main Market, Jor Bagh • 2469 7102

### Bharany's
Bharany's takes special pride in each and every one of its handcrafted jewellery items, but it also has a fine collection of textiles. ✎ Map R4 • 14, Sundar Nagar Market • 2435 8528

### Ladakh Jeweller's
A lovely shop that specializes in beautiful ethnic Indian handcrafted jewellery in gold and silver. ✎ Map R4 • 10, Sundar Nagar Market • 2435 5424

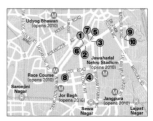

*Most shops in this area are open Mon–Sat, 10am–8pm.*

**Price Categories**

For a meal for one, including taxes and service charge but not alcohol.

® under Rs.200
®® Rs.200–500
®®® Rs.500–750
®®®® Rs.750–1,500
®®®®® over Rs.1,500

Bukhara, ITC Maurya Sheraton

# TOP 10 Places to Eat

**1 The Lodhi**
Like the hotel it is housed in, The Lodhi exudes chic style; it also serves up excellent Catalan cuisine. ® Map Q6 • The Aman, Lodi Road • 4363 3333 • Open daily noon–3pm & 7–11:5pm • ®®®®®

**2 Bukhara**
One of the world's top Indian restaurants, Bukhara serves superb North-West frontier cuisine. ® ITC Maurya Sheraton, Sardar Patel Marg • 2611 2233 • Open daily 12:30–2:45pm, 7–11:45pm • ®®®®®

**3 Sagar Ratna**
This place serves simple yet delicious vegetarian South Indian meals. ® Map L5 • The Ashok, 50 B, Chanakyapuri • 2688 8242 • Open daily 8am–11pm • ®®

**4 Threesixty Degrees**
A stylish place that brings Japanese, Italian, Mediterranean and Indian food under one roof. ® Map R5 • The Oberoi, Dr Zakir Hussain Marg • 2436 3030 • Open daily noon–3pm & 7–11pm • ®®®®®

**5 Baci**
One of the most charming spots in town, Baci has a strong Italian menu. ® Map R4 • 23, Sundar Nagar Market • 4150 7445 • Open daily 11am–midnight • ®®®®®

**6 Basil and Thyme**
Run by Bhicoo Manekshaw, the first Indian woman to have completed the advanced Cordon Bleu cookery course, this airy restaurant offers good European cuisine. ® Map L6 • Santushti Complex, Chanakyapuri • 2467 4933 • Open Mon–Sat 10:30am–6pm • ®®®®®

**7 Latitude**
This stylish café focuses on contemporary dishes with a twist. ® Map P5 • Good Earth, Khan Market • 2464 7175 • Open Mon–Sat 10am–6pm • ®®®®®

**8 Oberoi Patisserie and Delicatessen**
A swanky yet casual deli ideal for catching a quick bite with friends. ® Map R5 • The Oberoi, Dr Zakir Hussain Marg • 2436 3030 • Open daily 8am–9pm • ®®®®®

**9 The Big Chill**
The atmosphere here is warm, family-friendly and noisy with hearty Italian food. ® Map P5 • 68 A, Khan Market • 4157 7588 • Open daily noon–11:30pm • ®®®®

**10 Ploof**
A charming place serving wholesome dishes including excellent seafood. ® Map P6 • 13, Lodi Colony Market • 2464 9026 • Open daily 1:30pm–3.30pm & 7–11pm • ®®®

Around Town – South of the Centre

Left **Detail of the prayer hall screen, Qutb Complex** Right **Courtyard of the Quwwat-ul-Islam**

# South Delhi

THE UPWARDLY MOBILE SUBURBS OF SOUTH DELHI *are where you will find what makes modern Delhi tick, with a string of upmarket neighbourhoods, suave restaurants and glitzy modern malls. Despite its contemporary appearance however, South Delhi was home to the city's earliest settlements, and boasts many of the its most atmospherically time-warped monuments. Most date back to the Delhi sultans, whose various forts, mosques and mausoleums still stand scattered majestically amongst modern suburbia. The highlight is the extraordinary Qutb Minar complex and the adjacent Mehrauli Archaeological Park, while there are further memorable attractions at Tughlaqabad and Hauz Khas.*

*Mihrab of Sultan Garhi's Tomb*

## 🔟 Sights

1. Qutb Minar
2. Quwwat-ul-Islam
3. Mehrauli Village and Archaeological Park
4. Baha'i Temple
5. Ashoka's Rock Edict
6. Hauz Khas
7. Begumpuri Masjid
8. Chiragh Delhi
9. Tughlaqabad
10. Tomb of Sultan Ghari

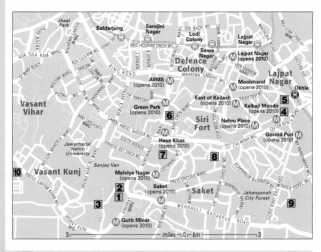

### 1 Qutb Minar

One of Delhi's most iconic sights, the soaring Qutb Minar towers over the southern city: a vast minaret begun during the reign of the first Delhi sultan Qutbuddin Aibak. The design is quite unlike anything else in the subcontinent, more Afghan than Indian, with angular projecting flanges punctuated by balconies and bands of Koranic script – a rugged and monumental memorial to the military and religious fervour of the first Delhi sultans (see pp18–19).

### 2 Quwwat-ul-Islam

The centrepiece of the Qutb Minar complex, the Quwwat-ul-Islam was the subcontinent's first mosque, begun by Aibak and extended by his successors; Alauddin Khilji (see p38), who added the fine Alai Darwaza red sandstone gateway in 1311. Inside the superb prayer hall screen, covered in profuse Koranic carvings, is one of India's finest early examples of Islamic architecture (see p18).

### 3 Mehrauli Village and Archaeological Park

The Mehrauli Archaeological Park and adjacent village of Mehrauli are home to an extraordinary

The towering Qutb Minar and Alai Darwaza

collection of ancient monuments, dating from the 12th to the 19th century. There is a rich cluster of Mughal monuments, ranging from the Jamal-Kamali Masjid to the Zafar Mahal, as well as notable Sultanate-era attractions such as the Jahaz Mahal and the serene *dargah* of the Sufi saint Qutb Sahib, buried away in the depths of the village (see pp20–21).

### 4 Baha'i Temple

Completed in 1986 to a design by Iranian architect Fariborz Sahba, the Baha'i Temple is Delhi's most striking modern building. Popularly known as the Lotus Temple, the design was inspired by the image of an unfolding lotus flower, with 27 enormous white petals emerging from nine pools, symbolizing the nine spiritual paths of the Baha'i faith. ⊗ *Map X2 • Kailash Colony • Open Mon–Sat summer: 9am–7pm, winter: 9:30am–5:30pm • www. uga.edu/bahai/india.html*

The beautiful Baha'i Temple in the evening

### Ashoka's Rock Edict

**5** Not far from the Baha'i Temple lies a large boulder, carved with a faint tracery of fading Brahmi script. This is one of the city's three monuments dating from the time of the Mauryan Emperor Ashoka *(see p56)*. Ashoka converted to Buddhism early in his reign, and erected a series of pillars and rock edicts across the country on which his various proclamations were recorded. Unlike the city's two Ashokan columns, this rock edict stands on its original site. ✆ *Map X2 • Off Raja Dhirsain Marg • Open 24 hrs*

Shops lining a street in Hauz Khas Village

### Hauz Khas Village

**6** The upmarket village of Hauz Khas is home to a string of ancient monuments, a Deer Park *(see p56)* and a number of eating and shopping venues. The village is centred around a reservoir, the Hauz-i-Alai, built by Alauddin Khilji in 1304. The sequence of buildings girding the lake were added half a century later by Feroz Shah Tughlaq. ✆ *Map U2 • Hauz Khas Village • Taxi, auto-rickshaw or Hauz Khas Metro • Open 24 hrs*

### Begumpuri Masjid

**7** This monumental mosque is a perfect example of the sturdy, fortress-like architecture

### Urban Villages

Scattered amidst South Delhi's suburbs are the remains of many formerly isolated villages which have now been swallowed up by the advancing urban tide. The most notable are Nizamuddin, Chiragh and Mehrauli. Each is home to an important *dargah* and retains its original street layout.

that was the fashion during the reign of the powerful Tughlaq sultans. Undeniably impressive, it features a huge arcaded courtyard topped by dozens of miniature domes, centred on the prayer hall's enormous *iwan*. ✆ *Map V2 • Vijay Mandal Enclave • Taxi, auto-rickshaw or Malviya Nagar Metro • Open daily sunrise–sunset*

### Chiragh Delhi

**8** Now engulfed by suburban sprawl, the ancient village of Chiragh Delhi has managed to preserve much of its traditional atmosphere, retaining parts of the walls that once surrounded it. The main attraction here is the *dargah* of Roshan Chiragh Delhi, while the stocky tomb of Delhi sultan, Buhlul Lodi, lies just outside the village. ✆ *Map W2 • Off Gamal Abdel Nasser Marg • Taxi or auto-rickshaw*

Dargah of Roshan Chiragh Delhi

**The remains of Tughlaqabad Fort**

## Tughlaqabad

Constructed during the reign of Ghiyasuddin Tughlaq *(see p38)*, Tughlaqabad was the third city of Delhi, dwarfing the previous settlements of Siri and Lal Kot, with a string of massive fortified ramparts and city walls stretching for 6 km (4 miles). The massive city walls and fortified citadel within are now largely ruined, but still hugely impressive. Just over the road lies the austere and unusual tomb of Ghiyasuddin himself. ◎ *Map X3 • Mehrauli Badarpur Road • Taxi, auto-rickshaw or Badarpur Metro • Open daily sunrise–sunset • Adm and charge for video*

## Tomb of Sultan Ghari

Marooned on the outskirts of the city, this impressive but little-visited tomb was built by Iltutmish for his son and heir Nasiruddin Mahmud following the latter's premature death in 1231. This is the oldest Islamic tomb in India, looking more like a fort than a mausoleum. The name Sultan Ghari means "Royal Cave", referring to the troglodytic burial chamber beneath the central octagonal platform. The tomb is an architectural curiosity, as much Hindu as Muslim in style. ◎ *Map T3 • Abdul Gaffar Khan Marg, Vasant Kunj • Taxi or auto-rickshaw • Open 24 hrs*

## A Day in South Delhi

### Morning

South Delhi's attractions are very spread out, and you will need to take transport between the various sites. You could pick up auto-rickshaws between each stop, though it is easiest to hire a knowledgeable taxi- or auto-rickshaw-driver for the day to ferry you around the various sites.

Start the day with an hour or so at the remarkable **Qutb Minar Complex**, then spend the rest of the morning exploring the monuments of the **Mehrauli Archaeological Park** and the adjacent **Mehrauli Village**. Next, head to the excellent **Garden of Five Senses** *(see p57)* and have lunch at **Magique** *(see p99)*.

### Afternoon

After lunch, head north, taking in some of Delhi's least-visited but most absorbing monuments, including the **Begumpuri Masjid**. Stop in the fascinating urban village of **Chirag Delhi** to visit the *dargah*. If you have time, visit the **Khirki Masjid** and nearby **Lal Gumbad** *(see p42)*. Then, drive over towards **Hauz Khas**. Visit the beautiful reservoir and surrounding buildings, the Deer Park, and then explore the quiet streets of Hauz Khas Village and its superb boutique shops. Continue north to the **Baha'i Temple** (aiming to arrive after 4pm, when the temple opens). Finally, make your way back to Nehru Place to the International Trade Tower for a meal at **Oh! Calcutta** *(see p98)*.

Left **Bar at Indian Accent** Right **Cool, classic decor at Aangan**

# 🔟 Places to Eat (Indian)

### 1 Swagath
Swagath serves the most delicious South Indian fare in town; their seafood is especially good. ◈ *Map W1 • 14, Main Market, Defence Colony • 2433 0930 • Open daily 11am–midnight • ₹₹₹₹*

### 2 Oh! Calcutta
Exuding old-world charm, this restaurant specializes in excellent traditional Bengali fare. ◈ *Map W2 • HA 1, International Trade Tower, Nehru Place • 646 4180 • Open daily noon–3pm; 7–11:15pm • ₹₹₹₹*

### 3 Punjabi by Nature
This friendly restaurant is most famous for its vodka *gol gappas* (puffed flour crisps filled with cumin-spiced water). ◈ *Map T1 • 11, Basant Lok, Vasant Vihar • 4151 6666 • Open daily noon–11:30pm • ₹₹₹₹*

### 4 Sagar
A friendly, canteen-style place, with reasonably priced, delicious vegetarian South Indian cuisine. ◈ *Map W1 • 18, Main Market, Defence Colony • 2433 3110 • Open daily 8am–10:30pm • ₹₹*

### 5 Indian Accent
A swanky yet cosy new place, offering finely prepared fare. ◈ *Map X2 • Manor Hotel, 77 Friends Colony • 2692 5151 • Open daily noon–3pm, 7pm–11pm • ₹₹₹₹₹*

### 6 Dakshin
Elegant and unassuming, this place serves the best Malayali food in the city.
◈ *Map V3 • Sheraton New Delhi Hotel, District Centre, Saket • 4266 1122 • Open daily 12:30–3pm; 7:30–11pm • ₹₹₹₹₹*

### 7 Zaffran
A stylish terrace space with simple but delicious food. ◈ *Map W2 • 2, N Block Market, Greater Kailash I • 4163 5000 • Open daily noon–3:30pm; 7:30pm–midnight • ₹₹₹₹*

### 8 Moksha
Dig into succulent mutton shammi kebabs, or gingery curd kebabs at Moksha. ◈ *Map X1 • 8, Community Centre, New Friends Colony • 4167 2777 • Open daily 12:30–3:30pm; 7:30pm–midnight • ₹₹₹₹*

### 9 Aangan
A quiet spot with a lovely courtyard serving traditional North Indian fare with a twist. ◈ *Map U1 • Hyatt Regency, Bhikaji Cama Place • 2679 0234 • Open daily noon–2:30; 7–11:30pm • ₹₹₹₹₹*

### 10 Gunpowder
This offers excellent Kerala cuisine as well as a fine view of the Hauz Khas reservoir. ◈ *Map U2 • 22, Hauz Khas Village • 2653 5700 • Open daily noon–4pm; 7–11pm • ₹₹₹*

**Price Categories**
For a meal for one, inclusive of taxes and service charge but not alcohol.

® under Rs.200
®® Rs.200–500
®®® Rs.500–750
®®®® Rs.750–1,500
®®®®® over Rs.1,500

Left **Chive and cashew dumplings at The Yum Yum Tree** Right **China Kitchen**

# 🔟 Places to Eat (Global)

### 1 The China Kitchen
A culinary milestone when it comes to good Chinese food in the city. ◎ Map U1 • Hyatt Regency, Bhikaji Cama Place • 2679 1234 • Open daily noon–3pm; 7–11:30pm • ®®®®®

### 2 Manré
A spacious restaurant with opulent dining areas and a fabulous European menu. ◎ Map V3 • MGF Metropolitan Mall, Saket • 4066 8888 • Open daily noon–3pm; 8pm–1am • ®®®®®

### 3 Diva
This quiet, understated little restaurant arguably serves the best Italian food in town. ◎ Map W2 • M 8, Main Market, Greater Kailash II • 2921 8522 • Open daily 1:30am–3:30pm; 7:30pm–midnight • ®®®®®

### 4 Tamura
Popular with expats, this cosy restaurant serves home-style Japanese fare. ◎ Map T1 • 8, D Block Market, Poorvi Marg, Vasant Vihar • 2615 4082 • Open daily noon–3pm; 6:30–10:30pm • ®®®®

### 5 The Yum Yum Tree
A blend of kitsch and Gothic, this makes for a fun Chinese meal among friends. ◎ Map X1 • Community Centre, New Friend's Colony • 4260 2020 • Open daily noon–3:30pm; 7pm–midnight • ®®®®

### 6 Smoke House Grill
A chic joint that serves modern European fare and focuses on smoked and grilled meats. ◎ Map W2 • LSC Masjid Moth, Greater Kailash II • 4143 5530 • Open daily 7:30–11:30pm • ®®®®®

### 7 Magique
A perfect place for a romantic meal under the stars. ◎ Map V3 • The Garden Village, Garden of Five Senses, Saidulajab • 2953 6767 • Open daily 7:30–11:30pm • ®®®®®

### 8 ai
An über-chic Japanese joint with excellent food that is now all the rage in the capital. ◎ Map V3 • MGF Metropolitan Mall, District Centre, Saket • 4065 4567 • Open daily noon–3pm; 7:30pm–midnight • ®®®®®

### 9 La Piazza
Fresh, hearty Italian dishes amidst relaxed, rustic surroundings. ◎ Map U1 • Hyatt Regency, Bhikaji Cama Place • 2679 1234 • Open daily noon–2:30pm; 7–11:30pm • ®®®®

### 10 Olive Bar & Kitchen
Located in an atmospheric haveli (old mansion), Olive serves up light Italian and Mediterranean fare. ◎ Map U3 • Kalkadas Marg, Haveli 6–8, One Style Mile, Mehrauli • 2664 4780 • Open daily • ®®®®®

Recommend your favourite restaurant on **traveldk.com**

Left **Abraham & Thakore store** Centre **Sculpture at Viya** Right **Ravissant**

# Top 10 Places to Shop

### 1 Viya
Everything is beautiful in Viya, which stocks gorgeous handcrafted furniture, hand-beaten metal accessories and sculpture, all inspired by Indian style through the ages. ✪ *Map U3 • 369, MG Road • 6528 8824 • Open Mon–Sat*

### 2 Nalli
Established in 1928, Nalli is now synonymous with exquisite silk saris in lovely colours and patterns. ✪ *Map V1 • 44, F Block, South Extension I • 2374 7154 • Open Tue–Sun*

### 3 Utsav
Utsav stocks saris in every possible fabric imaginable; it also has Indo-Western apparel, bags and footwear. ✪ *Map W2 • 3, Krishi Vihar Complex, Josip Broz Tito Marg • 2624 2420 • Open Mon–Sat*

### 4 Kilol
A lovely store specializing in hand-block-printed, reasonably priced fabrics from Jaipur. ✪ *Map W2 • 6, N Block Market, Greater Kailash I • 2924 3388 • Closed Tue*

### 5 Fabindia
Fabindia stocks everything from furniture and natural cosmetics to organic food and clothes. ✪ *Map W2 • 7, N Block Market, Greater Kailash I • 2923 2183 • 10am–8pm*

### 6 Zaza
A lovely lifestyle store filled with beautiful furniture, brightly coloured linen, unusual cutlery

and home decor products. ✪ *Map W2 • 25–26, Community Centre, Zamrudpur • 2923 5076 • Open daily*

### 7 Amaatra
A small jewellery store known for its beautiful designs. ✪ *Map V2 • 120, Shahpur Jat • 98101 94670 • Open Mon–Sat*

### 8 Ravissant
A sophisticated store with beautiful "Indian-inspired" clothes in breezy fabrics, home decor and silverware. ✪ *Map X1 • 50–51, Community Centre, New Friends Colony • 2632 8648 • Open Mon–Sat*

### 9 Abraham & Thakore
A Delhi fashion institution best known for its classic cuts and pristine natural fabrics. ✪ *Map T3 • 322 A, DLF Emporio Mall, Vasant Kunj • 4606 0995 • Open Mon–Sat*

### 10 Tatsat
Tatsat sells garments, accessories and stationery, all sourced from eco-friendly organizations. ✪ *Map U2 • E 50, Main Market, Hauz Khas • 4165 5792 • Open Mon–Sat; Sun noon–9pm*

Old-fashioned English charm at the Polo Lounge, Hyatt Regency

# 🔟 Bars and Cafés

### 1 Polo Lounge
Sink into a Chesterfield around the cosy fireplace and step back in time at this plush, England-inspired bar. ◈ *Map U1 • Hyatt Regency, Bhikaji Cama Place • 2679 1234 • Open daily 11am–12:30am*

### 2 Kylin
With fantastic cocktails, this is ideal for a lazy drink at lunch or a lively evening with friends. ◈ *Map T1 • 24, Basant Lok, Vasant Vihar • 4166 9778 • Open daily noon–midnight*

### 3 ai, The Love Hotel
A beautiful outdoor terrace bar, decked out with springy cushions and ambient lighting. ◈ *Map V3 • MGF Metropolitan Mall, District Centre, Saket • 4065 4567 • Open daily 7:30pm–midnight*

### 4 The Living Room Café
There is usually a live music performance on every other evening at The Living Room Café. ◈ *Map U2 • 1, Hauz Khas Village • 4608 0533 • Open daily 11am–midnight*

### 5 Hard Rock Café
Recently opened, the Hard Rock Café packs in the crowds, especially when there is a live band playing. ◈ *Map V3 • M 110, DLF Place, District Centre, Saket • 4715 8888 • Open daily noon–1am*

### 6 Shalom
Live music, paired with cool Mediterranean decor and great cocktails, make Shalom one of the city's most popular nightclubs. ◈ *Map W2 • 18, N Block Market, Greater Kailash I • 4163 2280 • Open daily 12:30–3:30pm; 7:30pm–midnight*

### 7 Café Turtle
Located atop Full Circle bookstore, this friendly café is a great place to unwind. ◈ *Map W2 • 8, N Block Market, Greater Kailash I • 2924 5641 • Open daily 10:30am–8:30pm*

### 8 Café Intermezzo
A quiet, home-style café with rotating art displays on the walls. ◈ *Map W1 • 34, Defence Colony Market • 2433 8119 • Open daily 10am–10pm*

### 9 Urban Pind
This dimly lit lounge attracts young professionals and expats with its cocktails. ◈ *Map W2 • 4, N Block Market, Greater Kailash I • 3251 4646 • Open daily 12:30pm–midnight; Wed: media and expat night*

### 10 Haze Blues and Jazz Bar
A great place to relax with a beer while listening to some excellent blues bands. ◈ *Map T1 • 8, Basant Lok, Vasant Vihar • 4166 9008 • Open daily 3pm–midnight*

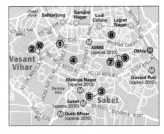

*Kylin hosts a ladies night and cocktail-making classes on Thursdays.*

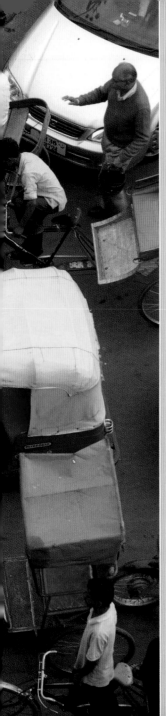

# STREETSMART

Planning Your Trip
104

Getting There
and Around
105

Sources of Information
106

Practicalities
107

Banking and
Communications
108

Security and Health
109

Things to Avoid
110

Shopping Tips
111

Accommodation Tips
112

Dining and Drinking Tips
113

Places to Stay
114–119

DELHI'S TOP 10

Left **Delhi Tourism Logo** Centre **Government book store, Connaught Place** Right **Traffic in the city**

# TOP10 Planning Your Trip

## 1 Passports and Visas

Citizens of all countries (except Nepal and Bhutan) require a visa to enter India. Contact your nearest consulate or embassy and allow plenty of time, especially if you are submitting an application by post. Check the following for more information: www.hcilondon.net (UK), www.indianembassy.org (USA), www.hciottawa.ca (Canada), www.hcindia-au.org (Australia) and www.hicomind.org.nz (New Zealand).

## 2 Tourist Information

Indian Government Tourist Offices can be found at: 7 Cork St, London (020 7437 3677; Suite 204, 3550, Wilshire Blvd, Los Angeles (213 380 8855); Suite 1808, 1270 Ave of Americas, New York, 10020 (212 586 4901); 60 Bloor St, West Suite 1003, Toronto (416 962 3787); Level 5, 135 King St, Glasshouse Shopping Complex, Sydney (02 9221 9555). The official website is www.incredibleindia.com.

## 3 When to Go

Between October and March daytime temperatures are pleasantly warm but not overpowering. Temperatures soar from April to September, while intermittent monsoon downpours can bring the city to a complete halt during July and August.

## 4 Weather

Daytime temperatures in Delhi range from the low 20°Cs (68°F) in winter up to the high 30°Cs (86°F) in summer. Winter nights can be surprisingly chilly; take a sweater.

## 5 Where to Stay

For casual visitors, the best place to stay is in or around Connaught Place. This lies more or less at the heart of the city, roughly equidistant from Old Delhi and Rajpath, and at the centre of the metro system. There are also plenty of restaurants, bars and shops in this area. For a cheaper but less salubrious alternative, head to the hotels of Arakashan Road, near New Delhi Railway Station, or the adjacent backpacker enclave of Paharganj. More expensive options are dotted all around the city, especially in South Delhi.

## 6 How Long to Stay

You could dash around all the headline sights in Delhi in about four days, although this wouldn't be a very relaxing experience. A week offers the chance to explore the city at a more leisurely pace and visit some of its more off-beat spots. Serious students of Indian history and architecture could spend a month or longer in the city without exhausting its many monuments.

## 7 What to Pack

There isn't much you can't buy in Delhi, but it is best to bring any necessary electrical equipment *(see below)* with you, along with a first aid kit. If you are staying in cheaper accommodation it may be useful to bring your own padlock and a universal sink plug.

## 8 Time Zone

The whole of India is in one time zone, known as IST, or Indian Standard Time. IST is 5 hours 30 minutes ahead of GMT, 10 hours 30 minutes ahead of US east coast time, 13 hours 30 minutes ahead of US west coast time, and 4 hours 30 minutes behind Sydney.

## 9 Insurance

Don't travel without valid insurance, and make sure you check the details of the policy, particularly how much you can claim for the loss of individual items.

## 10 Electrical Current and Adaptors

Electrical current is 220–240 volts AC, the same as in Europe, but double that of North America. Almost all wall sockets are designed for plugs with three round pins. Square-pin British and Australian appliances will just need an adaptor, while North American appliances will need a transformer as well.

Left **Central Secretariat metro sign** Centre **Bus interior** Right **Auto-rickshaw**

# TOP 10 Getting There and Around

### 1 By Air from Europe
There are direct, non-stop flights to Delhi from several European cities, and innumerable one-stop options. The best connections are from London Heathrow, which has direct flights with BA, Virgin Atlantic and Jet Airways.

### 2 By Air from North America
From the east coast the quickest way to fly is via Europe and the Gulf; from the west coast. It is a similar distance whether you fly via Europe or the Pacific. Most flights will involve one or more stops, although there are currently non-stop flights to Delhi from New York (Continental and Air India) and Chicago (Jet Airways and American Airlines).

### 3 By Air from Asia and Other Parts of India
There are numerous domestic airlines in India offering cheap flights between Delhi and every major city in the country. There are also direct connections with most other Asian capitals, as well as numerous points in the Gulf.

### 4 Overland from Neighbouring Countries
It is currently possible to travel overland into India from Pakistan, Nepal, Bangladesh and Bhutan, but not from China or Burma. There are no ferry services to India from Sri Lanka; you will have to fly.

### 5 Getting Around by Metro
Delhi's metro system is the most convenient way of getting around town. Trains runs every two to four minutes and tickets cost Rs.22 per journey ("smart cards" are also available, saving time and money if you are a frequent metro user). There are three lines: the Yellow line running north–south, and the Red and Blue lines running east–west. A number of metro line extensions are currently underway in time for the 2010 Commonwealth Games.

### 6 Getting Around by Bus
Delhi has a good bus network, although it is not very useful for casual visitors, with its array of routes and crowded vehicles. You can check routes online at: http://delhigovt.nic.in/dtcbusroute.

### 7 Getting Around by Taxi
Delhi's black-and-yellow-top taxis wait for custom at taxi ranks around the city. Check fares at: www.delhitrafficpolice.nic.in/auto-taxi-fare.htm. Make sure the driver uses the meter. Alternatively, you can hire a car and driver through your hotel, with rates from around Rs.700–800 per day.

### 8 Getting Around by Auto-rickshaw
This is the standard way of getting around Delhi. All rickshaws are fitted with meters, with fares set at Rs.4.50 per km, plus Rs.10 for the first km (full details at www.delhitrafficpolice.nic.in/auto-taxi-fare.htm). You can also hire pre-paid rickshaws at official metered rates from the small kiosks scattered around the city. Unfortunately, most drivers absolutely refuse to use their meters and you will probably end up having to haggle. Make sure you agree on a fare before setting off.

### 9 Getting Around by Cycle-rickshaw
These are slow, relatively uncomfortable and best avoided if you are in a hurry, but they are also cheap, eco-friendly and a great way of seeing parts of the old city. Fares are about half those of an auto-rickshaw. Note that cycle-rickshaws are banned from Connaught Place and certain other parts of New Delhi.

### 10 Getting Around on Foot
Delhi is very spread out, and the crowds and traffic can make walking seem unappealing. However, most of New Delhi is quite pedestrian-friendly, and the bazaars of the old city are fascinating to explore on foot.

Left **Magazines about Delhi** Centre **Delhi Tourism's office, Connaught Place** Right **Newspapers**

# 10 Sources of Information

## 1 Maps
The superb Eicher City Map street atlas covers the entire city in brilliant and reliable detail and is widely available. An alternative is the Freytag & Berndt New Delhi map, which is only slightly less detailed but only goes as far south as Safdarjung's Tomb.

## 2 Useful Websites
Useful sites include the Delhi Tourism and Transport Development Corporation (DTTDC) (www.delhitourism.nic.in) and the Archaeological Survey of India (ASI) (www.asi.nic.in); http://thedelhiwalla.blogspot.com is great for offbeat views of the city. Delhi Live (www.delhilive.com) and India for You (www.indfy.com) also cover local sights.

## 3 Other Useful Websites
For eating, drinking, shopping and events have a look at http://delhi.burrp.com; Time Out Delhi (www.timeoutdelhi.net) and Delhi Events (www.delhievents.com). For general Delhi- and India-related information, www.indiamike.com is the leading online forum.

## 4 City Tourist Offices
The office of the Delhi Tourism office (DTTDC) is at Middle Circle, Block N-36, Bombay Life Building, Connaught Place (open Mon–Sat 9am–6pm; 5152 3073). Note that there are many non-official offices masquerading as the DTTDC nearby. The Government of India tourist office is at 88 Janpath (open Mon–Fri from 9am–6pm, Sat 9am–2pm; 2332 0005).

## 5 Regional Tourist Offices
Rajasthan Tourism Development Corporation, 1st Floor, Bikaner House, Pandara Road (2338 3837; delhi@rtdc.in; www.rajasthantourism.gov.in); Uttar Pradesh Tourism, 36, Chandralok Building, Janpath (2335 0048; www.up-tourism.com). Haryana Government Tourist Bureau, 36, Janpath, Chandralok Building (2332 4910), http://haryanatourism.gov.in). Punjab Tourist Office, Kanishka Shopping Plaza, Ashoka Road (2332 3025, www.punjabtourism.in).

## 6 Listings Magazines
For listings of local events refer to Delhi City or First City. Delhi Diary, available free from the Government of India tourist office and many hotels, is also useful.

## 7 Newspapers
India has an excellent English-language press, with a wide range of newspapers and dailies. The most famous are The Times of India (whose local edition includes the Delhi Times supplement), The Hindu and the more free-thinking Indian Express.

## 8 Specialist Guidebooks
Lucy Peck's superb Delhi: A Thousand Years of Building has detailed descriptions and brilliant maps of virtually every place in the city. Giles Tillotson's Mughal India is a good companion to the Mughal monuments of Delhi and Agra. Old Delhi: Ten Easy Walks by Gaynor Barton and Laurraine Malone is also useful.

## 9 Tours and Guides
Whistlestop morning and afternoon tours are arranged by the DTTDC; alternatively, they can also put you in touch with registered local guides. Many hotels and travel agencies run similar tours, though the range can be rather stereo-typical. If you want to get off the beaten tracks buy the Eicher City Guide.

## 10 Gay and Lesbian
The 148-year-old rule prohibiting same-sex relationships was finally overturned in a landmark ruling in July 2009. Although there is still a considerable stigma attached to gays and lesbians in India, attitudes in Delhi are as liberal as anywhere in the country. Useful resources include: http:gaydelhi.tripod.com; www.indiandost.com/gay.php.

Left **No smoking sign** Centre **Indian currency** Right **Public convenience** *(sulabh)*

# 🔟 Practicalities

### 1 Opening Hours
Most shops are open Mon–Sat 10am–6pm. Banks are usually open Mon–Fri 10am until mid-afternoon and a few hours on Saturday mornings. Many museums and some other tourist sights are closed on Mondays.

### 2 Public Holidays
There are only four public holidays in the year with fixed dates that are observed all over India: Republic Day (26 Jan), Independence Day (15 Aug), Gandhi's birthday (2 Oct) and Christmas (25 Dec). Many other festivals, with variable dates, are celebrated.

### 3 Smoking Regulations
In late 2008, India introduced nationwide legislation prohibiting smoking in all public buildings, including restaurants, cafés, bars, shops, malls and offices. You are still allowed to smoke in outdoor areas.

### 4 Embassies and Consulates
The consular officials in Delhi can re-issue passports, and assist in case of theft, imprisonment, hospitalization or other emergencies.

### 5 Tipping and Baksheesh
For tipping in restaurants, cafés and hotels, 10 per cent is a good rule of thumb. Some places add a 10 per cent "service charge" to cover this. The Indian concept of *baksheesh* can mean anything from a tip given in thanks, to a bribe.

### 6 Weights and Measures
India follows the metric system (introduced between 1955–62), although old British measures are still occasionally employed. Two idiosyncratic Indian numbers that are used are the *lakh* (one hundred thousand, written 1,00,000) and the *crore* (ten million, or 1,00,00,000, usually abbreviated to cr).

### 7 Public Restrooms
There are relatively few public toilets *(sulabh)* in Delhi, and the ones that exist are fairly unsavoury (there is a small fee for using them). It is usually best to head to the nearest reputable hotel or café and use the facilities there.

### 8 Currency
The Indian currency is the Rupee, divided into 100 paise (although these are now rarely used). Notes come in denominations of Rs.10, 20, 50, 100, 500 and 1,000, while coins come in denominations of 1, 2, 5 and 10. Be careful not to accept torn or damaged banknotes, and be aware that change is usually in short supply.

### 9 Etiquette
Delhi has a reputation for being the rudest city in India, but a smile and a few polite words can be more effective than raising your voice. Shake hands and touch your food with your right hand only, remove your shoes when entering places of worship (and cover your head in Muslim shrines and Sikh *gurudwaras*). Dressing conservatively is recommended and couples should avoid embracing in public.

### 10 Beggars
Beggars mainly hang out around major road intersections, importuning passing vehicles for alms. Others are likely to be found in the vicinity of places of worship.

### Embassies in Delhi

**Australia**
4139 9900 • www.india.embassy.gov.au

**Canada**
4178 2000 • www.canadianinternational.gc.ca

**New Zealand**
2688 3170 • www.nzembassy.com

**UK**
2687 2161 • http://ukinindia.fco.gov.uk/en

**USA**
2419 8000 • www.newdelhi.usembassy.gov

Left **ATM, Indian Bank** Centre **South Indian Bank sign** Right **GPO, Baba Kharak Singh Marg**

# 10 Banking and Communications

### 1 Banking Hours
Banks are usually open Mon–Fri 10am until mid-afternoon, plus a couple of hours on Saturday mornings.

### 2 Currency Exchange
Most mid- and upper-range hotels will exchange foreign currency, although rates are often poor. There is a useful branch of Thomas Cook in Connaught Place offering better rates, plus various other Forex bureaux around the city. *Block C-33; Connaught Place • Closed Sun*

### 3 Traveller's Cheques
All banks (as well as Thomas Cook) change traveller's cheques, although be sure to check commission rates and any other hidden extras before handing them over. American Express, Thomas Cook and Visa cheques are the most widely recognized and easiest to convert.

### 4 ATMs
Be aware that your home bank or credit-card provider will probably apply additional charges. There are ATMs all over the city, as well as in most metro stations. The majority of these now accept foreign-issued credit and debit cards with Visa and MasterCard (although relatively few accept American Express or Diner's Club). ATMs are generally the easiest

way of accessing funds, and tend to offer good exchange rates.

### 5 Credit Cards
Visa and MasterCard are widely accepted in most upmarket shops and restaurants. Note, however, that paying by credit card may attract a surcharge of between two and seven per cent, and be aware of the risks of credit-card fraud in less reputable establishments.

### 6 Post Offices
There is a handy branch post office in Connaught Place. For *poste restante*, you will need to go to the GPO (General Post Office) at the intersection of Baba Kharak Singh Marg and Ashoka Road, also near Connaught Place. If you are receiving a letter, make sure it is addressed to "Poste Restante New Delhi GPO", or it will end up at the Old Delhi GPO on Mahatma Gandhi Road. *Block A–6; Connaught Place • 2336 4111• Closed Sun*

### 7 Internet Access
Some mid-range and virtually all top-end hotels provide Internet (often WiFi) access – albeit sometimes at exorbitant rates, especially in the five-star international chains. There are plenty of independent Internet cafés dotted around the city, and an increasing

number of the city's smarter cafés now provide free WiFi as well.

### 8 Telephones
International and national phone calls can be made easily and relatively cheaply from the numerous telephone booths dotted around the city (look for places advertising STD/ISD phone calls). Calls can often be made from hotel rooms too, although there may be an extortionate mark-up; check rates before calling.

### 9 Mobile Phones
If you are planning on using your mobile while in Delhi, check rates and accessibility with your service provider at home (most US phones, except Tri-Band phones, won't work in India). Alternatively, you can buy a SIM card from an Indian telecom provider (available at phone shops), which will give you an Indian phone number and access to extremely cheap local phone rates.

### 10 Television
Most hotel rooms in Delhi now come with TV, offering a variety of local and international channels. The leading local broadcaster is Star TV, including movie and sports channels, plus Zee TV. You are also likely to get ESPN sports, CNN and BBC news channels and a variety of other offerings.

*The country phone code for India is +91, and the regional code for Delhi is 011.*

Left **Vehicle, Delhi Police** Centre **Chemist** Right **Woman shopper at Janpath**

# ¹⁰⁰ Security and Health

### ¹ Crime
The good news is that violent crime against visitors to Delhi is rare. The bad news is that petty theft is fairly common, albeit no worse than in any other Asian metropolis. Pickpocketing and theft from hotel rooms are the most common complaints.

### ² Security Tips
For tips on hotel security *(see p112)*. The risk of pickpocketing *(see p110)* can be minimized by carrying all valuables in secured bags rather than loose in pockets, and by slinging bags over your neck and carrying them in front of you (backpacks are inherently less safe). Many travellers use money belts, although these are not necessarily secure. It is also a good idea (for women travellers especially) to exercise due caution after dark.

### ³ Police
If you need the police in an emergency, call 100. Besides its regular force, Delhi also has a dedicated corps of tourist police, although petty thefts are not likely to elicit a proactive response.

### ⁴ Emergency Phone Numbers
For the fire brigade call 101 and for an ambulance, 102. There are plans to introduce a new India-wide emergency number (108) covering all three services, though this has yet to be launched in Delhi.

### ⁵ Women Travellers
The major hassle faced by women travellers to Delhi is the so-called "Eve teasing" *(see p110)*. Solo women may also attract friendly, if not necessarily welcome, attention in parts of the city. The best advice is to dress conservatively and to exercise reasonable caution after dark.

### ⁶ Crossing Roads
Given the heavy traffic, crossing busy roads is likely to be the most dangerous thing you do in Delhi. Always exercise caution and expect the unexpected, such as cyclists, motorbikes and auto-rickshaws heading the wrong way down the road. If in doubt, find a group of locals and cross the road with them.

### ⁷ Vaccinations
Meningitis, typhoid, tetanus and hepatitis A vaccinations are all commonly recommended for travellers to India; you should also make sure that you are covered against polio. Exactly what you will need will depend on where you are going. Consult your doctor or a specialist travel health clinic for expert advice, well before your trip.

### ⁸ Insect-Borne Diseases
India's two major mosquito-borne diseases, malaria and dengue fever, are relatively rare in Delhi, although outbreaks do occur with potentially life-threatening consequences. Both are most common in and following the monsoon months (Jul–Sep), when virus-carrying mosquitos breed in stagnant water.

### ⁹ Food and Water Safety
The majority of visitors to Delhi experience no health problems whatsoever, although a few common-sense rules will increase your chances of enjoying a healthy stay. Stick to bottled drinking water (or purify your own) and avoid food that looks stale – the busier and more popular the restaurant, the safer it is likely to be. Street food can play havoc with delicate constitutions, and ice cream, salads and peeled fruit are all notorious germ-carriers.

### ¹⁰ Delhi-Belly, Giardia and Dysentery
The most common illness suffered by visitors here is Delhi-Belly – a stomach upset that passes within a day or two (stick to water, yoghurt and rice). If symptoms persist, consult a doctor in case you have contracted giardia or amoebic dysentery.

Left **Cow in the middle of a road** Centre **Street food carts** Right **Rush-hour traffic**

# 🔟 Things to Avoid

### 1 Contaminated Food and Water
You should not get paranoid about falling ill when in Delhi; most food and drink in the city is fine. However it is worth sticking to bottled water and exercising caution over what you eat and drink (see p109).

### 2 Rush-Hour Traffic
Delhi's traffic can be bad at any time, but is particularly horrible during the morning and evening rush-hours. The metro also fills up at these times, with queues forming at ticket counters and security checkpoints. Avoid travelling during this time if you can.

### 3 Hard-Sell Auto-rickshaw Drivers
Haggling over fares with auto-rickshaw drivers can be a tedious business. Even worse is when, having agreed a price, they start trying to take you to a shop of their choosing en route in order to extract some extra commission. Taxi drivers can also be guilty of this.

### 4 Aggressive Animals
There are not many animals in Delhi, but try to steer clear of stray dogs, which can occasionally turn aggressive. Temple monkeys, too, may look cute, but can deliver a bite if provoked. Wandering cows are safer, and it is considered auspicious to touch the rump of a holy cow.

### 5 Recreational Drugs
India is a major drug producer, and cannabis, opium and other substances are widely available, although still strictly illegal. Visitors (and foreigners above all) are particularly at risk of being ripped-off or set-up by unscrupulous dealers, especially in and around Paharganj. Visitors who are caught face, at best, a hefty bribe or, at worst, a long stint inside an Indian prison.

### 6 Eve Teasing
So-called "Eve teasing" (a euphemism for sexual harassment) is unfortunately not unknown in India's big cities. The perpetrators are usually teenage boys or young men. Eve teasing can range from making lewd remarks or catcalls, to "accidentally" bumping into women or brushing against them, or instances of groping in crowded places. The best response, if there are other people around, is to point out the perpetrator and explain in a loud voice exactly what he has done. The majority of people in Delhi will share your repulsion.

### 7 Pickpockets
Delhi is generally a safe place, although petty crime exists here as in any other major city. Crowded streets, trains and buses offer good cover for pickpockets. Make sure your valuables are secured and in sight.

### 8 Hotel Thefts
Thefts (or minor pilfering) in cheaper hotel rooms are fairly common. The best solution is to use your own padlock where possible (although most Delhi hotel rooms have key locks). Hotels should have a safe to store valuables, although it is not unknown for things to go missing out of these either. The only truly reliable solution is to keep everything in a locked suitcase, and then chain the suitcase to the bed.

### 9 Drugged Food
Although extremely rare, there are occasional instances of visitors to India being offered drugged food or drink and then robbed once insensible. Be wary of accepting edibles or drinks from strangers.

### 10 Credit Card Fraud
Credit card fraud is widespread in India. The most common scam is to take your credit card out of your sight and swipe multiple impressions of it, which can then be signed later at will. Try to ensure that your credit card is swiped in front of you and that it never leaves your sight.

Left **Traditional textiles** Centre **Bargains at Sarojini Nagar Market** Right **Kamala, Connaught Place**

# 🔟 Shopping Tips

## 1 Bargaining

Bargaining is essential in all bazaars and most smaller shops (but not usually malls, government emporiums and more upmarket places). Buying expensive or multiple items should always help lower prices; alternatively try saying you have seen a similar item elsewhere at a cheaper price. If all else fails, make to leave the shop, which often triggers further discounts. If it does not, you can always go back later.

## 2 Government Emporiums

The city's extensive range of official state emporiums on Baba Kharak Singh Marg display artifacts from all over the country at fixed, marked prices. They are generally good places to shop: quality is usually reliable and the prices are not outrageous. Even if you do not buy anything, it is worth visiting to check out the full range of handicrafts and get a rough idea of prices before heading off elsewhere.

## 3 Bazaars

For more mainstream articles – such as shoes, clothing, jewellery and electronics – the city's innumerable old-style bazaars are often the best places to shop – and also the most fun. Bargaining is essential, with the possibility of big discounts if you strike lucky.

## 4 Malls and Designer Shops

Shopping in the city's smart malls and branded shops is a very different experience from bargaining in the bazaars. On the plus side, prices are generally marked, quality assured and it is possible to browse without being hassled. On the down-side, prices are notably higher and bargaining is not an option.

## 5 Commission Rackets

The city's auto-rickshaw drivers are a major source of shopping hassle. They will often try to take you to an inferior shop where they collect commission on anything you buy. Such places are best avoided.

## 6 Crafts

There is a wide array of crafts available from all over India. The state government emporiums are the best places to start looking, while the Crafts Museum, Dilli Haat, Industree and Sundar Nagar Market also have excellent selections.

## 7 Religious Artifacts

For a truly authentic Indian souvenir, consider some of the city's colourful and often quirky religious artifacts. Good collectibles include traditional metal and wooden statuettes, and bright posters of Hindu deities. There is also an interesting array of Islamic paraphernalia available, particularly at Meena Bazaar (see p12), just in front of the Jama Masjid.

## 8 Textiles

Hundreds of shops sell textiles by the metre; anything from fine Benarasi silks to home-spun cotton (khadi). Look out for rugs, Rajasthani wall hangings, silk table-cloths, or have material made into clothes.

## 9 Clothing

Delhi is brilliant for clothes, from the relatively upmarket, but still very affordable, local chains such as Anokhi and Fabindia, through to innumerable bargain offerings in clothing bazaars such as the Tibetan Market off Janpath near Connaught Place, Katra Neel off Chandni Chowk, or Paharganj. Alternatively, buy some fabric and have your clothes tailored at affordable prices.

## 10 Jewellery

For jewellery, head to the colourful Dariba Kalan, just off Chandni Chowk in Old Delhi, which has dozens of shops selling silverware, gold and precious stones. There are also excellent jewellery shops in many of the city's modern malls and quieter shopping enclaves such as Hauz Khas Village and Shahpur Jat.

Left **Room at Amarya Haveli** Right **Reception at Hotel Palace Heights**

# 10 Accommodation Tips

### Price Categories

Accommodation in Delhi can be surprisingly expensive. If money is no object there are some fine places to stay, including ritzy establishments run by leading five-star hotel chains and some alluring boutique hotels. Otherwise the choice is fairly limited, with most budget accommodation found near New Delhi Railway Station, either in the establishments of Paharganj (largely aimed at foreign backpackers) or the slightly more upmarket hotels of nearby Karol Bagh.

### Finding a Hotel

Check reputable guidebooks and browse online: www.tripadvisor.com can be useful and gives a comprehensive overview of what is available, as long as you take the user reviews with a pinch of salt. It is also worth checking the reviews at www.indiamike.com/india-hotels

### Choosing a Location

Delhi is very spread out, and it is useful to think about what you plan to do there before picking a hotel. A place near a metro station is a definite plus if you plan on using public transport. The best area, overall, is in or around Connaught Place, which puts you more or less in the heart of the city, within easy reach of

an excellent range of restaurants, cafés, bars and shops; though accommodation here generally comes with a mark up.

### Online Discounts and Offers

Always check online for special offers or Internet discounts if you are planning to stay at one of the city's upmarket hotels.

### Hotel Amenities

A good hotel can provide you with much more than a place to sleep; amenities such as an efficient in-house travel desk, restaurant and bar can make your stay a lot more pleasant. You might also want to check whether there is room service, what the smoking policy is and whether the hotel serves alcohol, Internet facilities, and any other useful features; for instance, in summer, a swimming pool is priceless.

### Check Rooms in Advance

Most hotels have a wide range of rooms of varying standards. Always have a look at your room before checking in, or better still, ask to see several rooms.

### Check for Cleanliness

In cheaper hotels, take nothing for granted. The first priority is to check the room's overall

cleanliness and general state of maintainance. Avoid rooms with grimy sheets, holes in the walls and peeling plaster.

### Check the Fittings

Make sure that any fans and air conditioners (if provided) work and don't make a horrible noise, that hot water (if provided) also works, and that the mattress is not rock hard. It is also worth checking how many lights there are, and how many actually work. Keep an eye out for unreliable, or unsafe electrical equipment such as television sets.

### Check for Noise

Noise is another potential problem. Always aim for a room around the back or sides of a hotel, away from the main road. Check for other sources of noise, such as nearby cafés and shops. Rooms near elevators, stairways and cleaning cupboards also tend to be noisy; the quietest rooms are usually at the ends of corridors.

### Hidden Extras and Haggling

Check whether the quoted room tarrif includes all taxes and service charges. You might also want to try haggling for a discount, especially if business looks quiet or if you will be staying for several nights at the hotel.

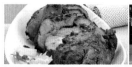

Left **Indian cuisine at Legends of India** Right **Drinks lined up along the bar in Rick's**

# 🔟 Dining and Drinking Tips

### 1 Indian is Best
It may sound obvious, but the best food in Delhi is Indian. Although there are a few upmarket exceptions, by and large you are most likely to eat well if you stick to Indian dishes, rather than trying the versions of European or Chinese food offered at the city's various multi-cuisine restaurants.

### 2 Go Regional
There is much more to subcontinental cuisine than the stereotypical Anglo-Indian menus served abroad (and even in Delhi itself). The city has some superb regional restaurants specializing in little-known cuisine from across the sub-continent; try Punjabi by Nature *(see p98)*, Oh! Calcutta *(see p98)*, or the excellent, cheap South Indian food served up in the citywide Saravana Bhavan chain *(see p77)*.

### 3 Go Vegetarian
The meat served in Delhi restaurants, especially in lower-end places, often consists of more bone and sinew than actual flesh. You will often get better food by going vegetarian; the universal Indian staple of *paneer* (cottage cheese) is a particularly good alternative to meat, and almost universally tasty. Spicy chickpeas *(channa masala)* are another reliable, tasty and widely available option.

### 4 Mughlai Cuisine
If you eat in Agra, be sure to sample the city's celebrated Mughlai cui-sine, perfected during the reign of the Mughal emperors. The style of cooking uses creamy, delicately spiced sauces, with dried fruit and nuts. You will also find tradi-tional Mughlai dishes in many restaurants in Delhi.

### 5 Indian Sweets
Although these are something of an acquired taste, Delhi is the perfect place to sample the art of the Indian sweet-maker. Ghantewala in Chandni Chowk *(see p11)* has been in business since the Mughal era and is a particularly good place to explore local confectionary.

### 6 Hygiene
Although it is easy to overstate the possible perils of Delhi-Belly (most visitors experience no problems), it is still worth keeping an eye on hygiene when eating. Salads, fruit and ice cream are particularly notorious germ-carriers, and it is best to avoid buffets, and street food that looks stale.

### 7 Street Food
Stalls all over the city dish up dirt-cheap and often tasty street food. Be aware, though, if you are not used to Indian street cooking, that hygiene standards at such places can some-times leave a certain amount to be desired.

### 8 Drink With the Jet Set
For a taste of the urban glitz of contemporary Delhi and the chance to rub shoulders with some of the city's beautiful people, go out for a cock-tail at one of its many upwardly mobile bars *(see pp66–7, 79, 101)*.

### 9 Coffee Time
Over the past few years, European-style café culture has arrived in Delhi with a vengeance, and the city now boasts a string of cosy, air-condi-tioned cafés offering pastries, juices and freshly brewed coffee. These are the perfect places to relax over a cappuccino and cake, unwind with friends, or even read a book. Barista, Café Coffee Day and Costa Coffee are the three main chains.

### 10 Information
There is a huge number of restaurants in Delhi, with new places opening all the time. For the latest news and reviews, check out http://delhi.burrp.com (on which restaurants, cafés and bars can be searched either by area or types of cuisine). The website www.timeoutdelhi.net is also worth a look for its detailed and unbiased restaurant reviews.

Left **Visitor using the WiFi facility at YMCA** Right **Ginger Hotel, New Delhi Railway Station**

# 🔟 Budget Hotels

### 1 YMCA
Established in 1927, the YMCA hostel continues to provide budget accommodation to foreign and local visitors to Delhi. The rooms, while basic, are, more importantly, clean and have en suite bathrooms. There is an in-house cyber café and a restaurant serving traditional Indian food. ◈ *Map F7 • Jai Singh Road, Connaught Place • 2336 1915 • www.newdelhiymca.org • ⑱⑱*

### 2 International Youth Hostel
Given its price and location, it is no wonder that the Youth Hostel is a huge favourite among young budget travellers. You can choose from dormitories with A/C, or double rooms with a shared or private toilet. ◈ *Map K5 • 5, Nyaya Marg, Chanakyapuri • 2611 6285 • www.yhaindia.org • ⑱*

### 3 Blue Triangle Family Hostel (YWCA)
The objective of the Blue Triangle is to provide safe and clean accommodation, particularly for women. It has grown in popularity over the last few years. There is a choice of double or single rooms, all of which are reasonably clean and comfortable and have en suite baths with running hot water. ◈ *Map E7 • Ashoka Road • 2336 0133 • www.ywcaofdelhi.org • ⑱*

### 4 Ginger Hotel
Winner of the CNBC travel award for the Best Budget Hotel, Ginger is located at the higher end of the budget spectrum. The rooms are spotlessly clean and there is a gym, a WiFi zone and a restaurant. ◈ *Map G5 • IRCTC – Rail Yatra, New Delhi Railway Station, Bhav Bhutti Marg • 6663 3333 • www.gingerhotels.com • ⑱*

### 5 Hotel Tara Palace
The Tara Palace may not receive kudos for its appearance but it has friendly service and is located bang in the heart of Old Delhi, making it perfect for exploring this chaotic yet charming area, with the Jama Masjid and Red Fort within walking distance. ◈ *Map H4 • 419, Esplanade Road, Chandni Chowk • 2327 6465 • www.tarapalacedelhi.com • ⑱*

### 6 Hotel New Haven
This hotel has a relatively nice location and clean rooms. Visitors are advised not to eat in though; head across to M Block market for a wider choice of meals. ◈ *Map W2 • E 512, Greater Kailash II • 2921 8556 • www.nhh.in • ⑱⑱*

### 7 Prince Polonia
One of the most popular higher-end budget hotels, the Prince Polonia offers unexciting yet relatively clean rooms amid the bustle of Paharganj. Connaught Place is within walking distance. ◈ *Map F5 • 2325–26, Tilak Gali, Chuna Mandi, Paharganj • 4762 6600 • www.hotelprincepolonia.com • ⑱*

### 8 Metropolis Tourist Home
Due to its excellent location and friendly service, the Metropolis has fast become a popular budget option among backpackers. Located in the middle of busy Paharganj, it also has a nice rooftop terrace restaurant. ◈ *Map F5 • 1634, Main Bazaar, Paharganj • 2356 1794 • ⑱*

### 9 Le Marlin
The rooms at Le Marlin are relatively clean and it offers efficient service. It is also well located in South Delhi, allowing easy access to the area's shops and sights. ◈ *Map W2 • D 55, East of Kailash • 4160 1010 • www.le-marlin.com • ⑱⑱*

### 10 South Delhi Cottage
Located on a relatively quiet road, South Delhi Cottage offers basic accommodation in a great location – for business travellers as well as tourists. The rooms are clean and spacious; try to get one with a balcony. ◈ *Map W2 • Opposite Nehru Place, Main Road • 6510 3320 • www.123hotelsdelhi.com • ⑱⑱*

*Room rates may vary according to season, availability and promotions. All prices listed are high-season rates.*

**Price Categories**

For a standard double room per night, including tax and service charges but not breakfast.

| ® | under Rs.2,000 |
| ®® | Rs.2,000–5,000 |
| ®®® | Rs.5,000–8,000 |
| ®®®® | Rs.8,000–15,000 |
| ®®®®® | over Rs.15,000 |

Left **Hotel Broadway lobby** Right **Double room in Hotel Palace Heights**

# TOP 10 Mid-Range Hotels

### 1 BB Palace

This is a clean, friendly place with pleasant, eager-to-please staff. The decor in some rooms borders on the tacky, but others are genuinely lovely with bold, bright colours coupled with dark wooden furniture. ✆ Bank Street, Gurudwara Road, Karol Bagh • 2875 1111 • www.hotelbbpalace.com • ®®

### 2 Ahuja Residency

Located in one of the most upmarket residential quarters in the city, this is a good option for a quiet, relaxing stay. Efficient, non-intrusive staff, beautiful room decor that blends the contemporary with the traditional, a cosy dining space, and all modern amenities make this a great home away from home. ✆ Map Q5 • 193, Golf Links • 2462 2255 • www.ahujaresidency.com • ®®®

### 3 27 Jor Bagh

27 Jor Bagh is a small, safe and charming spot located close to the beautiful Lodi Gardens, which is perfect for lazy afternoon picnics and evening strolls. The interior is simple, fuss-free yet comfortable and spotlessly clean. There is also a lovely lawn and a verandah area with wicker chairs to lounge in. ✆ Map N7 • 27, Jorbagh • 2469 4430 • www.jorbagh27.com • ®®

### 4 Centre Point

Despite its slightly run-down, old-world air, this place nevertheless offers good service and clean rooms. There is a 24-hour coffee shop in-house, as well as an option of walking across to one of the many restaurants in Connaught Place. ✆ Map G7 • 13, Kasturba Gandhi Marg, Connaught Place • 2332 4472 • ®®

### 5 Bajaj Indian Homestay

The rooms at the Bajaj Indian Homestay are named, in a rather gimmicky way, after Hindu gods and their avatars, and other mythological characters. They are clean and spacious and there is a charming rooftop terrace. ✆ 8A/34, Karol Bagh • 2573 6509 • www.indianhomestay.com • ®®

### 6 Hotel Broadway

Built in 1956 and sandwiched between Old Delhi and Connaught Place, this hotel has a certain endearing charm. The friendly staff arrange traditional dance performances and walking tours through the old city. ✆ Map H5 • 4/15-A, Asaf Ali Road • 4366 3600 • www.hotelbroadwaydelhi.com • ®®

### 7 Hotel Florence

A decent hotel offering comfortable rooms with clean en suite bathrooms. An in-house restaurant serves Indian and European dishes. ✆ 2719, Bank Street, Karol Bagh • 4714 4714 • www.hotelflorence.in • ®®

### 8 Hamilton Hotel

Located at the edge of quiet Panchsheel Park, the Hamilton is a good option from which to explore South Delhi. A number of the rooms are cheerfully done up in bright colours, and there is a charming verandah with wicker chairs and a fountain. ✆ Map V2 • S 153, Panchsheel Park • 2601 6124 • ®®

### 9 One Link Road

One Link Road is a small yet friendly place with a nice living room and a homely dining area with basic furniture. ✆ Map R7 • 1, Link Road, Jangpura Extension • 4182 4083 • www.onelinkroad.com • ®®

### 10 Hotel Palace Heights

The Palace Heights has many qualities to recommend it: a great location, an excellent in-house restaurant, and tastefully decorated rooms with lovely paper blinds and warm, woody colours. The softly-lit terrace restaurant is perfect for a beer and a plate of chicken tikka. ✆ Map F6 • D 26–28, Connaught Place • 4358 2610 • www.hotelpalaceheights.com • ®®®

Left **The B Nineteen living room with Humayun's Tomb in the background** Right **Casa Friends**

# TOP 10 Boutique Hotels

### Amarya Garden
Tucked away in quiet, leafy Defence Colony, Amarya Garden is a four-room urban hideaway housed in an elegant white Colonial mansion. The service is friendly and non-intrusive while the rooms, all tastefully done up in various colour schemes, are understated yet luxurious. ⊗ *Map W1 • C 179, Defence Colony • 4656 2735 • www. amaryagroup.com • ®®®® (including complimentary breakfast)*

### Amarya Haveli
Located in a peaceful residential colony, Amarya Haveli (also run by the owners of Amarya Garden) has six rooms that range from glitzy Bollywood to Jaipuri pink. The star attraction of the place is the gorgeous roof-top restaurant. ⊗ *Map U2 • P 5, Haus Khas Enclave • 4175 9268 • www.amaryagroup.com • ®®® (including complimentary breakfast)*

### Thikana
The eight rooms in this warm, little hotel have an earthy feel about them – ethnic prints, dark furniture, and lots of maroons and browns. The two living rooms areas are well-equipped with comfortable chairs for you to sink into with a book or a drink. ⊗ *Map V2 • A 7, Gulmohar Park • 4604 1569 • www. thikanadelhi.com • ®®*

### Lutyen's Bungalow
Built in 1935, this charming bungalow is located in plush Central Delhi, strolling distance from Lodi Gardens and Safdarjung's Tomb. There is a swimming pool to soak in during summer and a living room with a fireplace and books for cold, winter evenings. ⊗ *Map N6 • 39, Prithviraj Road • 2461 1341 • www. lutyensbungalow.co.in • ®®® (including complimentary breakfast)*

### The Muse
Though not as atmospheric as most boutique hotels in this city, The Muse is excellent for business travellers as it is centrally located and close to the Nehru Place commercial complex. Their rooms are stylish but fuss-free. ⊗ *Map W2 • A 1, Chirag Enclave • 4065 0000 • www. musedelhi.com • ®®®®*

### B Nineteen
B Nineteen is a gorgeous boutique hotel with six vibrant rooms that blend tasteful contemporary style with traditional furniture and bright colours. The rooms have lovely wooden furniture coupled with striking linen, rugs and curtains. The service is non-intrusive and warm and the location top notch. ⊗ *Map S6 • B-19, Nizamuddin East • 4182 5500 • www.bnineteen. com • ®®®*

### Casa Delhi
Quiet, peaceful and overhung with plants and flowers, this lovely building will make you feel you are not in the heart of a city. ⊗ *Map W1 • C 56, Defence Colony • 99714 25558 • www. casaboutiquehotels.com • ®®® (including complimentary breakfast)*

### Casa Friends
Spread over two sprawling floors of a townhouse located in up-market Friends Colony, Casa Friends is an opulent choice of accommodation. ⊗ *Map X1 • C 62, Friends Colony • 99714 25558 • www.casaboutiquehotels. com • ®®®*

### The Residence
The 22 bedrooms at The Residence have beautiful handcrafted Burmese teak furniture, contemporary art on the walls and the rooms that are airy and comfortable. ⊗ *Map V2 • S 362, Panchsheel Park • 4050 2121 • www.justahotels. com • ®®®®*

### Colonel's Retreat
Calling itself Delhi's "best-kept secret", this charming accommodation option feels like you are staying in a friend's home. Slouch into their lazy-boy chair and watch television, or read a book. ⊗ *Map W1 • D 418, Defence Colony • 9999 720 024 • www. colonelsretreat.com • ®® (including breakfast)*

*Drop by the kitchen if you are staying at Amarya Garden to learn a few basic Indian recipes.*

## Price Categories

For a standard double room per night, including tax and service charges but not breakfast.

® under Rs.2,000
®® Rs.2,000–5,000
®®® Rs.5,000–8,000
®®®® Rs.8,000–15,000
®®®®® over Rs.15,000

Left **Luxury room at The Oberoi** Right **Suite at The Imperial**

# TOP 10 Luxury Hotels

### The Imperial
Opened in 1931, The Imperial is considered one of Asia's finest hotels. From its sweeping palm–lined drive off Janpath–to its classical white Colonial structure, the place exudes quiet elegance and luxury. The walls are lined with a fine collection of European "traveller" paintings. ⓢ Map F7 • 1, Janpath • 2344 1234 • www.theimperialindia. com • ®®®®®

### The Aman
The world-famous Aman chain has finally come to Delhi, and they have done it with their usual aplomb. Strong on modern, minimalist looks, the building effortlessly adds traditional touches like Mughal jali screens, Khareda stone floors and elaborate flower bowls, with sleek rooms. ⓢ Map Q6 • Lodi Road • 4363 3333 • www.amanresorts. com • ®®®®®

### The Claridges
A landmark in Lutyen's Delhi, Claridges is the epitome of old-world style. The building, characterized by Colonial pillars and high ceilings, houses 137 rooms and suites, a shopping arcade, and great restaurants. You will find it difficult to leave, as did the Beatles when they stayed here in 1968. ⓢ Map N5 • 12, Aurangzeb Road • 3955 5000 • www.claridges-hotels.com/delhi • ®®®®

### The Park
Contemporary art and design are the highlight of this hotel's decor. The Park is a treat with their impeccable service and chic, spacious rooms Unwind at Aqua, the terrace garden woven around a glittering swimming pool. ⓢ Map F7 • 15, Parliament Street • 2374 3000 • www. theparkhotels.com • ®®®®

### The Taj Mahal Hotel
This exclusive hotel has a gorgeous lobby complete with Art Deco patterned marble floors, fountains and beautiful mini-domes. The rooms are just as impressive, with decor that is a bold blend of traditional and contemporary. ⓢ 1, Man Singh Road • 2302 6161 • www.tajhotels.com • ®®®®®

### The Oberoi
Located in one of the poshest areas of the capital city, the Oberoi exudes tremendous grace and style. The highlights of staying here include spectacular views of Humayun's Tomb, especially when it is lit up at night. ⓢ Map R5 • Dr Zakir Hussain Marg • 2436 3030 • www.oberoidelhi. com • ®®®®®

### ITC Maurya
Despite its slightly Nehruvian architectural appearance, the ITC Maurya is a delightful accommodation option not only for its impeccable service but also for its location, its forested Ridge views and its excellent in-house restaurant Bukhara. ⓢ Diplomatic Enclave, Sardar Patel Marg • 2611 2233 • www. itcwelcomgroup.in • ®®®®®

### The Taj Palace
This grand building is nestled within lovely lawns and has striking interiors. Relax at the nine-hole putting green or work out at the state-of-the-art fitness centre. ⓢ Diplomatic Enclave, Sardar Patel Marg • 2611 0202 • www.tajhotels.com • ®®®®®

### Oberoi Maidens
Built in the early 1900s and nestled close to leafy Civil Lines, this beautiful white building, with its Colonial architectural style still retains a strong old-world charm. ⓢ Map G1 • 7, Sham Nath Marg • 2397 5464 • www. maidenshotel.com • ®®®®

### Hyatt Regency
The Hyatt is ideal for the traveller who likes to feel the vibrant pulse of the city. The imposing structure houses a flamboyant lobby space, stylish rooms, a sleek club lounge and some excellent restaurants. ⓢ Map U1 • Bhikaji Cama Place • 2679 1234 • www.delhi.regency.hyatt. com • ®®®®

Left **Room in His Grace B&B** Right **Terrace Garden, Vandana's B&B**

# TOP 10 B&Bs and Guesthouses

### 1 Maharani Guest House
The well-maintained Maharani Guest House is well-placed for exploring both South and Central Delhi. It is ideal for a quiet stay, away from the hustle and bustle of the city. ◈ *Map R4 • 3, Sundar Nagar • 2435 9521 • ®®*

### 2 Sai Villa B&B
Though not the most stylish, Sai Villa offers clean, spacious rooms, well-equipped en suite bathrooms, attentive staff and a prime location. The place also has tie-ups with a number of restaurants, so guests can order in meals as if at home. ◈ *Map W2 • E 578, Greater Kailash II • 4057 3242 • www.saivilla.com • ®®*

### 3 His Grace B&B
Located in upmarket Defence Colony, His Grace B&B is a comfortable option with spacious, well-equipped rooms. For meals or a drink, hop across to the local restaurant- and bar-packed market. ◈ *Map W1 • D 105, Defence Colony • 4657 8109 • ®®*

### 4 Delhi B&B
Delhi B&B is lovely, with bright, quirky furniture, green potted plants and lovely wall-hangings. Pervez and Lubna Hameed, the owners, are well-travelled and can converse fluently in French. They encourage their guests to watch the hostess prepare Indian meals, and can offer advice and tips on sightseeing and the city. ◈ *Map X1 • A 6, Friends Colony East • 98110 57103 • www.delhibedandbreakfast.com • ®®*

### 5 Vandana's B&B
This family-run B&B is a warm, cosy affair, and feels rather like staying with friends. The highlight is the charming rooftop garden, perfect for enjoying breakfast in the winter sun, or a chilled drink in the evenings while the city lights twinkle around you. ◈ *Map V1 • B 4/124, Safdarjung Enclave • 2618 6355 • www.bedandbreakfastnewdelhi.in • ®®*

### 6 Trendy B&B
Run by Madhu Taneja, a well-travelled hostess with a wide network of friends across the globe, Trendy B&B has something of a cosmopolitan feel. The rooms are spotlessly clean, spacious and uncluttered. ◈ *Map R7 • 9–B, Mathura Road, Jangpura • 9350 723 328 www.trendybb.com • ®®*

### 7 Dawar Villa B&B
Dawar Villa is a smart family-run B&B located in Bengali Market, a place which is famous for its eating joints. It is also close to Mandi House, one of the city's main cultural centres. The place has a warm feel to it, with gorgeous wood panelling, earthy colours and soft lighting. ◈ *Map G7 • 50, Todarmal Road, Bengali Market • 9911 321 555 • www.dawarvilla.com • ®® (including breakfast)*

### 8 On the House
On the House has seven rooms, named after trees, and done up in vivid colours. It prides itself on its homely feel, and the home-cooked food here is delicious. The B&B is a favourite with solo women travellers. ◈ *Map V1 • B 4/120, Safdarjung Enclave • 4602 4897 • www.bedandbreakfastnewdelhi.com • ®®*

### 9 11 Nizamuddin
Housed in an elegant Colonial bungalow with a mid-sized lawn, the rooms here are charming and uncluttered. The area is smart, peaceful and quiet, close to many parks and heritage monuments such as the beautiful Humayun's Tomb. ◈ *Map S6 • 11, Nizamuddin (East) • 2435 1225 • www.elevendelhi.com • ®®*

### 10 G 49 Nizamuddin
Tucked away in a leafy street, G 49 Nizamuddin is a relaxed, friendly place with elegant decor and spotless en suite rooms. The dining area and balcony space are attractive and sociable. ◈ *Map R6 • G 49, Nizamuddin (West) • 2435 0014 • www.bedbreakfast.asia • ®®*

*Speak to Mr Anand, the owner of 11 Nizamuddin, for first-time visitor information on Delhi.*

**Price Categories**

For a standard double room per night, including tax and service charges but not breakfast.

| | |
|---|---|
| ® | under Rs.2,000 |
| ®® | Rs.2,000–5,000 |
| ®®® | Rs.5,000–8,000 |
| ®®®® | Rs.8,000–15,000 |
| ®®®®® | over Rs.15,000 |

The beautiful pool area in The Oberoi Amarvilas, Agra

# TOP 10 Hotels Around Delhi

### 1 The Oberoi Amarvilas
Built in a Moorish- and Mughal-inspired style, this gorgeous hotel, located near the Taj Mahal, is steeped in extravagance and ethnic elegance. ® *Map C3 • Taj East Gate Road, Agra • 0562 2231 515 • www.amarvilas. com • ®®®®®*

### 2 Mughal Sheraton
This resort is a luxurious treat for the senses, not only due to its impeccable decor and service but also because it houses the country's largest spa – Kaya Kalp. After a tiring day's sightseeing, relax in a private *hamam* (Turkish bath). ® *Map C3 • Taj Ganj, Agra • 0562 4021 700 • www. itcwelcomgroup.in • ®®®®®*

### 3 Rambagh Palace
Built in 1835, Rambagh Palace seems to be a place that time forgot; known as the "Jewel of Jaipur", an air of royalty hangs around it with its arches, pristine walls, airy windows and lavish grounds. It has been voted one of the best hotels in the world by Conde Nast. ® *Map B3 • Bhawani Singh Road, Jaipur • 0141 2211 919 • www.tajhotels.com • ®®®®®*

### 4 Diggi Palace
Built around 1727, Diggi Palace is both charming and vibrant.

It hosts a number of cultural events, including the annual Jaipur Literary Festival, which draws in writers from all over the globe. The hotel itself is lovely, with peacocks in the garden, tinkling fountains and rooms that hint at a glorious past. ® *Map B3 • SMS Hospital Road, Jaipur • 01141 2373 091 • www.hoteldiggipalace. com • ®®*

### 5 Tiger Den
This state-run hotel is a great budget option for those who wish to visit the Sariska Wildlife Sanctuary (see p68). Speak to the staff about sightseeing and safari tours. ® *Map B3 • Sariska, Alwar • ®*

### 6 Neemrana Fort-Palace
Carved into a hillside, this architectural jewel is steeped in history and offers unparalleled elegance. Take a dip in the pool with an awesome view of the horizon, or pamper yourself with an ayurvedic treatment. ® *Map B3 • Delhi–Jaipur highway, Village Neemrana, Alwar • 01494 2460 06 • www.neemranahotels. com • ®®*

### 7 The Hill Fort
Located on a crop of rocks, this hotel offers splendid views of the surrounding countryside. Inside, the rooms are cool, with high ceilings, and delicately decorated

in traditional Mughal style. ® *Map B3 • Village Kesroli, near MIS post office, Bahala, Alwar • 01468 2893 52 • www. neemranahotels.com • ®®*

### 8 Kadamb Kunj
Kadamb Kunj is located close to the Keoladeo Ghana National Park (see p68), and a great place to stay for bird-watching. ® *Map C3 • NH 11, Fatehpur Sikri, Bharatpur • 05644 2201 22 • www.kadambkunj.in • ®®*

### 9 Glasshouse on the Ganges
Set on the banks of the Ganges in a fruit orchard belonging to the Maharaja of Tehri Garhwal, this hotel has six cottages overlooking the river and the mountains beyond. Among the activities available are white-water rafting, fishing (permit required) and trekking. ® *Map C2 • 23rd Milestone, Rishikesh–Badrinath Road, Village & PO Gular–Dogi • 09412 0764 20 • www. neemranahotels.com • ®®*

### 10 Ranjit's Svaasa
A family-run heritage hotel, Ranjit's Svaasa is housed within the walls of a 19th-century Colonial building. Everything here exudes elegance: from the lovely garden to the courtyard on to which the four suites open. ® *Map B1 • V 47-A, The Mall, Amritsar • 0183 2566 618 • www.svaasa.com/ranjit. com • ®®®*

# General Index

11 Nizamuddin 118
19 Oriental Avenue 77
1911 65, 75, 79
27 Jor Bagh 115

**A**

Aangan 98
Abraham & Thakore 100
accommodation
  B&Bs 118
  boutique hotels 116
  budget hotels 114
  guesthouses 118
  luxury hotels 117
  mid-range hotels 115
  hotels around Delhi 119
  tips 112
Adham Khan's Tomb 20, 60
Adiga, Aravind 58
Adilabad 38
Afsarwala Mosque and Tomb 14
Agni 75, 79
Agra Fort 13, 20, 32, 68
Ahuja Residency 115
ai, The Love Hotel 67, 101
Aibak, Qutbuddin 18, 36. 37, 43, 95
Ajmeri Gate 83
Akbar (emperor) 20, 24, 32, 33, 44, 68
Akbar Shah II (emperor) 21, 45
Akshardham Temple 52, 88, 89, 91
Alai Darwaza 19, 95
Ali, Ahmed 59
Amaatra 100
The Aman 117
Amar Jawan Jyoti 73
Amarya Garden 116
Amarya Haveli 116
Amir Khusrau 41, 53, 61, 90
Amrapali 92
Anangpal II 36
Andhra Pradesh emporium 62
Anokhi 92, 111
Aqua 66, 75, 79
Arab Serai 14
Archaeology Department of the Guru Gobind Singh Indraprastha University 48

Arjumand Banu Begum
  see Mumtaz Mahal
Arora, Manish 62
Ashoka Column 84
Ashoka (emperor) 84, 96
Ashoka's Rock Edict 96
Ataga Khan 44
Athpula 25
ATMs 108
Aulia, Kabiruddin 42
Aulia, Sheikh Nizamuddin 44, 51, 53, 61, 90
Aurangzeb (emperor) 8, 9, 11, 45
auto-rickshaw 105, 109, 111
Avalokitesvara 27

**B**

Babur (emperor) 15, 25, 33, 36, 37, 43
Baci 66, 93
Bahadur, Ahmad Shah 90
Bahadur, Teg 11
Bahadur Shah Zafar II (emperor) 37, 81
Baha'i Temple 52, 95, 97
Baha'u'llah 52
Bajaj Indian Homestay 115
Baker, Herbert 16, 17, 58, 76
Bakr, Abu 49
bakrikhani 65
baksheesh 107
Bal, Rohit 62
Balban's Tomb 20
Ballimaran 47, 60, 83
Banking hours 108
banks 107, 108
Bara Darwaza 61
Bara Gumbad Masjid 25
Bara Gumbad Tomb 24
The Barber's Tomb 15
bargaining 111
bars, cafés & nightclubs
  1911 79
  Agni 79
  ai, The Love Hotel 101
  Aqua 79
  Café Intermezzo 101
  Café Turtle 75, 101
  Cha Bar 79
  Hard Rock Café 101
  Haze Blues and Jazz Bar 101
  Kylin 101

bars, cafés & nightclubs (cont.)
  Legends of India Tea Terrace 79
  Polo Lounge 101
  Qashqai 79
  Q'Bar 79
  Rick's 79
  The Living Room Café 101
  Triveni Tea Terrace 79
  Sam's Café 79
  Shalom 101
  Urban Pind 101
Barton, Gaynor 106
Basil & Thyme 91, 93
Battle of Panipat 36
BB Palace 115
Beating the Retreat 40
Begum, Qudsia 56
Begumpuri Masjid 38, 42–3, 53, 96, 97
Begum Samru's Palace 10
Bhagwan Shri Swaminarayan 52, 89
Bharany's 92
Bhuta Sculpture Gallery 22
The Big Chill 75, 93
Bijay Mandal 38
bin Tughlaq, Muhammad 36, 37, 38, 43, 52–3
bird-watching 61
Birla House see Gandhi Smriti
The Black Taj 31
Blue Triangle Family Hostel (YWCA) 114
B Nineteen 116
boating 61
The Bookshop 92
Bose, Nandalal 55
Boutique hotels 116
British Residency 48
Brunch spots 65
Buddha Jayanti 41
Buddha Jayanti Park 56
Budget hotels 114
Bu Halima's Garden 14
Bukhara 64, 93
Burj-i-Shamali 9

**C**

Café Intermezzo 101
cafés see bars, cafés & nightclubs

Café Turtle 75, 101
Car Parts Bazaar 46
*Casablanca* (film) 66
Casa Delhi 116
Casa Friends 116
Central Cottage Industries
  Emporium 78
Centre Point 115
Cha Bar 75, 79
*Chak De* (film) 59
Chandni Chowk 6, **10–11**,
  47, 81, 83
  shopping 62
  walks around Delhi 60
*Chandni Chowk to China*
  (film) 59
Chauburji Masjid 84
Chauhan (dynasty) 38
Chauhan III, Prithviraj 36
Chawri Bazaar 47, 83
The China Kitchen 65, 99
Chini-ka-Rauza (Agra) 33
Chiragh Delhi 96
Chor Bizarre 85
Chowk-i-Jilo Khana (Taj
  Mahal) 30
churches
  Cathedral Church of the
    Redemption 16, 76
  Central Baptist Church
    10
  St James' Church 48,
    52, 80
*City of Djinns* (Dalrymple)
  58
city tourist offices 106
Claridges 117
classical music *see* music
*Clear Light of Day* (Desai)
  58
clothes 63, 111
cocktails 67
coffee time 113
Colonel's Retreat 116
commission rackets 111
communications 108
Connaught Place (CP)
  62–3, 73, 75
Coronation Park 57
Correa, Charles 22
crafts 63, 111
Crafts Museum 7, **22–3**,
  55, 74, 75, 111
Crafts Museum Shop 78
credit cards 108
crime 109
currency 108
The Curzon Room 85

cycle-rickshaw 105
cycling 61

**D**
Dakshin 98
*dal bukhara* (lentils) 64
Dalrymple, William 58, 59
Dancing Girl (National
  Museum) 26
Daniell, Thomas 55, 77
Daniell, William 77
Daniell's Tavern 77
Dara Shikoh (son of Shah
  Jahan) 27, 48
Dargah Qutb Sahib 20–21
Dariba Kalan 46, 60, 62,
  83
Daulatabad 36
Dawar Villa B&B 118
Dawat Khana 8, 83
*Delhi: Adventures in a
  Megacity* (Miller) 58
*Delhi: A Thousand Years of
  Building* (Peck) 106
Delhi B&B 118
Delhi-Belly 109, 113
Delhi Cycling Club 61
*Delhi Diary* 106
Delhi Golf Club 61
*Delhi 6* (film) 59
Delhi Noir (Sawhney) 59
Delhi Riding Club 61
Delhi Sultanate 18–19, 36,
  42, 43
*Delhi Times* 106
Delhi Zoo 89
Desai, Anita 58
designer shops 111
*Dev D* (film) 59
Dhrupad 51
Diggi Palace 119
Dilli Haat 63, 111
Dining and drinking tips
  113
discounts 112
Diva 99
Diwali 41
Diwan-i-Aam (Red Fort) 9
Diwan-i-Khas (Red Fort) 9
*dokra* art 62
drugged food 110
Dussehra 41

**E**
electrical current and
  adaptors 104
embassies 107
Embassy Restaurant 85

emergency phone
  numbers 109
Enoteca 67
eve teasing 110

**F**
Fabindia 62, 92, 100
*Fanaa* (film) 59
Fatehpuri Masjid 11, 48,
  81, 83
Fazlullah, Sheikh 20
F Bar & Lounge 66–7
Feroz Shah Kotla 39, 43,
  84
Ferozabad 38, 39, 43
festivals and events 40–41
*Fire* (film) 59
*First City* 106
Flagstaff House 54
Flagstaff Tower 48, 61
Flame of the Forest *(Butea
  monosperma)* 57
food poisoning
  contaminated food and
    water 110
foundation of New Delhi
  *see also* Lutyens, Edwin
Fraser, William 82
frisbee 61

**G**
galleries *see* Museums
  and Galleries
Gandharan Buddha 27
Gandhi, Indira 37, 43, 54,
  56, 74, 81, 82
Gandhi, Mohandas K. 37,
  53, 54, 56, 74, 81
Gandhi, Rajiv 54, 74, 81
Gandhi Smriti 54
Gandhi Smriti Museum 73
Ganesh Chaturthi 41
Ganga (goddess) 27
The Garden Terrace 85
Garden of Five Senses 57
Gauri (goddess) 10
Gauri Shankar Temple 10,
  60, 84
gay travellers 106
George V, King 56
Ghalib, Mirza 61, 84, 90
Ghantewala 11b, 83, 113
Ghata Masjid *see* Zinat ul
  Masjid
Ghazi-ud-Din 83
Ghori, Muhammad 18, 36
Giardia 109
Ginger Hotel 114

Girdhari Lal 78
Glasshouse on the Ganges 119
G 49 Nizamuddin 118
golfing 61
Good Earth 62, 92
Government Emporiums 111
guesthouses 118
Gujarati Samaj 85
Guliyan Bazaar 46
Gulmohar (Delonix regia) 57
Gunpowder 98
Gurgaon 39
Gurudwara Bangla Sahib 52, 76
Gurudwara Sisganj (Chandni Chowk) 11, 61
Guru Purab 41

**H**
Haldiram's 10, 83, 85
Halwai, Balram 58
Hamilton Hotel 115
Hanuman Mandir 76
Hard Rock Café 101
Hardy, Justine 58
Har Krishan, Sikh guru 52
Hauz-i-Alai 96
Hauz Khas Deer Park 56
Hauz Khas 38, 43, 60, 96–7
Hauz Khas Village 60, 63, 97, 111
Haveli Haider Quli 60
Hayat Bakhsh Bagh 8
Haze Blues and Jazz Bar 101
Hidden extras and haggling 112
Hill Fort 119
The Hindu 106
His Grace B&B 118
history 36–7
Hodson, William 49
Holi 40
horse riding 61
Hotel Broadway 115
Hotel Florence 115
Hotel New Haven 114
Hotel Palace Heights 115
Hotel Tara Palace 114
Humayun (emperor) 14, 15, 15b, 37, 39, 44, 89
Humayun's Tomb 6, **14–15**, 44, 89, 91
Hyatt Regency 117

**I**
Ibrahim Lodi 25b, 36, 43
Id-ul-Fitr 41
The IIC Experience 41
Iltutmish 19, 43, 97
The Imperial 117
Imperial City of the Mughals 33
Independence (1947) 37
India Gate 16, 39, 61, 73, 75
India Habitat Centre 24, 50, 51
India International Centre 41, 51
Indian Accent 98
Indian Express 58, 106
Indian laburnum (Cassia fistula) 57
Indian Mountaineering Foundation 61
Indian Temple Tree (Plumeria) 57
Indira Gandhi Memorial Museum 54, 73
Indraprastha 38, 39
Industree 78
insurance 104
Inter Continental 97
International Youth Hostel 114
Iron Pillar (Qutb Minar) 19
Islamic architecture 18–19, 42, 95
ITC Maurya 117
Itimad-ud-Daulah (Agra) 32, 68

**J**
Jacaranda 57
Jahanara, Princess 53, 90
Jahan-e-Khusrau 41
Jahangir 32, 44
Jahanpanah 38, 53
Jahaz Mahal 21, 60, 95
Jai Singh II, Maharaja of Jaipur 74
Jamali-Kamali Masjid 20
Jama Masjid (Agra) 32
Jama Masjid (Delhi) 7, **12–13**, 39, 44, 45, 46, 47, 52, 60, 81, 83
Jamat Khana Masjid 53
Jamun (Syzygium cumini) 57
Janpath 62
Jantar Mantar 74, 75

Jennings, Reverend Midgeley John 49
jewellery 63, 111
Joshi, Ruchir 59

**K**
Kabhi Khushi Kabhie Gham (film) 59
Kachnar (Bauhinia variegata) 57
Kadamb Kunj 119
Kake di Hatti 85
Kaki, Qutbuddin Bakhtiyar 20–21
Kali (goddess) 26
Kamala 78
Kamani Auditorium 50
Karim's 12, 65, 83, 85
Kashmiri Gate 49
Katra Neel 47
Kerala emporium 62
Khadi 78
Khair, Tabish 59
Khair ul-Manazil Masjid 90, 91
Khan, Afzal 33
Khan, Isa 15
Khan, Khizr 25b, 43
Khan, Mohammad Quli 20
Khan, Shahrukh 59
Khan-i-Khanan's Tomb 44, 90–91
Khan Market 62, 75
Khari Baoli 46–7, 83
Khas Mahal (Red Fort) 9
Khayal 51
Khilji, Alauddin (emperor) 18, 19, 37, 38, 43, 95, 96
Khirki Masjid 42, 97
Kilol 100
Kinari Bazaar (Agra) 32
Kinari Bazaar (Delhi) 46
Krishna Janmashtami 41
Kriti 51
Kylin 65, 67, 101

**L**
Ladakh Jeweller's 92
ladoos 11
Lahori Gate 8
Lakshmi Narayan Mandir 53, 73
Lala Chunna Mal's Haveli 11
Lal Darwaza 49
Lal Gumbad 42, 97
Lal Kot 36, 38, 97
Lal Mandir 10, 53, 60, 83

*The Last Mughal* (Dalrymple) 59
Latitude 75, 93
Legends of India 77
Legends of India Tea Terrace 79
lesbian travellers 106
*lingam* 10
literature 58–9
The Living Room Café 101
The Lodhi 64, 66, 93
Lodi, Buhlul (sultan) 43, 96
Lodi Gardens **24–5**, 43, 56, 60, 90, 91
Lodi, Sikander 24, 25, 43
Lodi dynasty 25b, 43
Lotus Eaters 62
Lotus Temple *see* Baha'i Temple
Lutyens, Edwin Landseer 17b, 37, 56, 73, 76
Lutyen's Bungalow 116
luxury hotels 117

**M**
Madhi Masjid 20
Madrasa of Alauddin Khilji 18
Magazine, Monument of the 1857 Uprising 48
Magique 97, 99
*Mahabharata* 38
Maham Angah 90
Maharani Guest House 118
Maha Shivaratri 41
Mahavir Jayanti 41
Mahmud, Nasiruddin 97
malls 111
Malone, Laurraine 106
Mandi House 61
Manre 65, 99
Mariam's Tomb (Agra) 33
Le Marlin 114
Medd, Henry 16
Meena Bazaar 12, 47, 60, 81
Mehra, Rakeysh Omprakash 59
Mehrauli 20, 21, 41
Mehrauli Archaeological Park 20, 60, 95, 97
Mehrauli Village 60, 95, 97
Mehtab Bagh (Agra) 32
Metcalfe, Sir Thomas Theophilus 20, 21, 82
Metcalfe's Folly 21b
metro 105

Metropolis Tourist Home 114
military parades 17
Miller, Sam 58
Mirza Ghalib Haveli 84
Mirza Ghiyas Beg 32
Mittal Tea House 92
Moksha 98
*Monsoon Wedding* (film) 59
Monuments of the 1857 Uprising 48–49
Mosaic 77
Moti Mahal 85
Moti Masjid 9
Mughal architecture 45
Mughal, Mirza 49
Mughal Emperor Shah Jahan in Dara Shikoh's Marriage Procession (painting) 27
Mughal Gardens 17, 56
*Mughal India* (Tillotson) 106
Mughal Sheraton 119
Mughlai cuisine 113
Muhammad Shah's Tomb 25
Mumtaz Mahal 30, 31
The Muse 116
Museums and Galleries
  Crafts Museum **22–3**, 55
  Gandhi Smriti 54
  Gandhi Smriti Museum 73
  Indira Gandhi Memorial Museum 54, 73
  National Gallery of Modern Art (NGMA) 55, 76
  National Gandhi Museum 54–5, 84
  National Museum **26–9**, 54, 73, 75
  National Philatelic Museum 55, 76
  National Rail Museum 55, 91
  Nehru Memorial Museum 54, 76
  Sikh Museum (Chandni Chowk) 11
  Sulabh International Museum of Toilets 55
music 51
Mutiny Monument 49

**N**
Nair, Mira 59
Nai Sarak 47
Nalli 100
Naqqar Khana 8
National Bonsai Garden 24
National Gallery of Modern Art (NGMA) 55, 76
National Gandhi Museum 54–5, 84
National Museum **26–9**, 54, 73, 75
National Philatelic Museum 55, 76
National Rail Museum 55, 91
Nehru Memorial Museum 54, 76
National School of Drama (NDS) 40, 50, 61
Neem *(Azadirachta indica)* 57
Neemrana Fort-Palace 119
Nehru, Jawaharlal (Prime Minister) 54
Nehru Memorial Museum 54, 76
Nehru Park 57
Neminatha 27
New Delhi 39, 72–5
  area map 76
  bars and cafés 79
  best of the rest 76
  foundation of 37
  restaurants 77
  shopping 78
*New Delhi: Making of a Capital* (Singh) 58
newspapers 106
Nicholson, Brigadier– General John 49, 84
Nicholson's Cemetery 49, 84
nightclubs *see* bars, cafés & nightclubs
Nila Gumbad 15
Nizamuddin 44, 51, 53, 61, 90, 91
Northern Ridge 48, 61, 84
Nur Jahan 32

**O**
The Oberoi 117
The Oberoi Amarvilas 119
Oberoi Maidens 117
Oberoi Patisserie and Delicatessen 93

Ogaan Closet 92
Oh! Calcutta 65, 97, 98
Old Delhi **80–83** *see also*
  Shahjahanabad
  area map 86
  best of the rest 84
  restaurants 84
*Old Delhi: Ten Easy Walks*
  (Barton and Malone) 106
Olive Bar & Kitchen 64, 99
One Link Road 115
One Style Mile 64
On the House 118
outdoor activities

**P**
Padam 51
Paranthe-wali Gully 10, 85
The Park 117
parks and gardens
  Buddha Jayanti Park 56
  Coronation Park 57
  Garden of Five Senses
    57
  Hauz Khas Deer Park 56
  Lodi Gardens **24–5**, 43,
    56, 60, 90, 91
  Mehtab Bagh (Agra) 32
  Mughal Gardens 17, 56
  National Bonsai Garden
    24
  Nehru Park 57
  Qudsia Bagh 56, 84
  Raj Ghat 56, 81
  Rambagh Gardens
    (Agra) 33
  Talkatora Gardens 56
  Urdu Park 12
Parsi Anjuman Hall 51
passports 104
Peacock Throne 9
Peck, Lucy 106
People Tree 78
La Piazza 65, 99
Phool Walon ki Sair 41
picnic 61
Pipul (*Ficus religiosa*) 57
Pir Ghaib 84
Ploof 93
Police 109
polo 61
Polo Lounge 67, 101
Polonia, Prince 114
post offices 108
Prayer Hall (Jama Masjid)
  13
Prayer Hall Screen
  (Qutb Minar) 19

price categories 112
public holidays 107
Punjabi By Nature 65, 98
Purana Qila 15, 39, 44, 61,
  89, 91
Purani Dilli Havelis 60

**Q**
Qala-i-Kuhna Msajid 89
QashQai 75, 79
Q'Bar 75, 79
Qila Rai Pithora 36, 38
Qudsia Bagh 56, 84
Quli Khan's Tomb 20, 21b
Qutb Festival 41
Qutb Minar 7, **18–19**, 20,
  38, 41, 42, 65, 95, 97
Quwwat-ul-Islam 18, 42,
  95

**R**
Rahim, Abdur 44, 90
Raisina Hill 17, 40, 76
Rajdhani 77
The Rajiv Gandhi
  Handicrafts Bhavan 62
Rajon ki Bain 21
Raj Ghat 56, 81
Rajpath **16–17**, 73, 75
Rama Navami 41
*Ramayana* 41, 46, 57
Rambagh Gardens (Agra)
  33
Rambagh Palace 119
*Rang de Basanti* (film) 59
Rang Mahal (Red Fort) 9
Ranjit's Svaasa 119
Rashtrapati Bhavan 17, 56,
  73, 75
Ravissant 100
recreational drugs 110
Red Fort 6, **8–9**, 39, 44,
  60, 81, 83
Red Silk Cotton Tree
  (*Bombax ceiba*) 57
Regional Tourist Offices
  106
The Residence 116
Republic Day Parade 17,
  40
restaurants 64–5, 113
  New Delhi 77
  Old Delhi 84
  South Delhi 98–9
  South of the Centre 92
restrooms 107
Rick's 66, 79
rock climbing 61

Roshan Chiragh Delhi,
  dargah of 96
Round Tower (Lodi
  Gardens) 25
Russell, Robert Tor 75

**S**
Sabz Burj 15
Safdarjung, Nawab of
  Awadh 90
Safdarjung's Tomb 45, 90,
  91
Sagar 98
Sagar Ratna 65, 93
Sahba, Fariborz 95
Sahib, Qutb 41, 95
Sai Villa B&B 118
Sakura 65
Sam's Café 79
Sangeet Natak Akademi
  50
Sansad Bhawan 16, 75, 76
Santushti 62
Saravana Bhavan 77
Sarojini Nagar 63
Sawhney, Hirsh 59
Sayyid dynasty 25b, 43
*Scoop-wallah: Life on a
  Delhi Daily* (Hardy) 58
Sealy, Irwin Allan 59
Secretariat Buildings 17,
  39, 75, 76
security 109
seekh kebabs 65
Select Citywalk Complex
  63
Shah, Muhammad 90
Shah, Nadir 19
Shah Burj (Red Fort) 9
Shahjahanabad 8, 36, 39
Shah Jahan (emperor)
  8, 37
  Agra Fort 32
  Chandni Chowk 10, 11
  Jama Masjid 13b
  Mughal Emperor Shah
    Jahan in Dara Shikoh's
    Marriage Procession
    (painting) 27
  Red Fort **8–9**
  Safdarjung's Tomb 45
  Shahjahanabad 36, 39
  Taj Mahal 30–31
Shalom 101
Shanti Vana 81
Sher Mandal 61, 89
Sher Shah Suri 15, 37, 39,
  44, 89

Shish Gumbad (Lodi Gardens) 25
The Shop 78
shopping 62–3, 111
    New Delhi 78
    South Delhi 100
    South of the Centre 93
Shri Ram Center for Performing Arts 50
Sikander Lodi's Tomb (Lodi Gardens) 24
Sikandra (Agra) 33, 68
Sikh Museum (Chandni Chowk) 11
Silverline 92
Singh, Malvika 58
Siri 38
Siri Fort 51
Skinner, James 52, 82
Smoke House Grill 99
smoking regulations 107
South Delhi 94–7
    bars and cafés 101
    restaurants 99–100
    shopping 100
South Delhi Cottage 114
South of the Centre 88–91
    restaurants 92
    shopping 93
The Spice Route 64, 77
spices 63
State Emporia Complex 62
Stein, Aurel 27
street food 113
Suddhadhana, King 26
Sulabh International Museum of Toilets 55
Sultan, Kizr 49
Sultan, Razia 43, 82
Sultan Ghari 97
Sundar Nagar Market 91
Sunehri Masjid (Chandni Chowk) 11
Summer Theatre Festival 40
Surajkund Crafts Mela 40–41
Surajkund 36, 40
Swagat 98
swimming 61

T
Tahliani, Tarun 62
Taj Ganj 30
Taj Mahal 7, 30–31
The Taj Mahal Hotel 117
Taj Nature Walk (Agra) 32

Talkatora Gardens 56
The Taj Palace 117
Tamura 99
Tapas Bar 66
Tarana 51
Tatsat 100
Tavernier, Jean-Baptiste 31b
taxi 105
tea 63
Teen Murti House 54
telephones 108
television 108
textiles 63, 111
thefts 110
Thikana 116
Things to avoid 110
Threesixty Degrees 65, 93
Tibetan Curios 78
Tiger Den 119
Tillotson, Giles 106
Times of India 106
time zone 104
Timur the Lame 36
tipping 107
Tomars dynasty 36, 38
Tomb of Ghiyasuddin Tughlaq 42
Tomb of Iltutmish 19
Tomb of Imam Zamin 19
Tomb of Maulana Azad 12
Tomb of Razia Sultan 82
Tomb of Sultan Ghari 97
Tomb of the Unknown Soldier (India Gate) 16, 73
tourist information 104
tourist offices 104
tours and guides 106
The Tower of Babel 19b
Town Hall (Chandni Chowk) 11
transport
    air 105
    auto-rickshaw 105
    buses 105
    taxis 105
travellers' cheques 108
Trendy B&B 118
tribal art 22
Tribes of India 62, 78
Triveni Kala Sangam 51, 61
Triveni Tea Terrace 75, 79
Tughlaq, Feroz Shah (emperor) 38, 43, 84, 96
Tughlaq, Ghiyasuddin 38, 42, 43, 97

Tughlaqabad 38, 42, 97
Tughlaq dynasty 36
Turkman, Hazrat Shah 82, 83
Twilight in Delhi (Ali) 59

U
Ugrasen's Baoli 76
Urban Pind 101
Urdu Park 12
Utsav 100

V
vaccinations 109
Vandana's B&B 118
Varq 64, 77
Veda 77
vegetarian restaurants 65, 113
Vijay Chowk 17, 40, 73
Vintage Car Rally 40
Vir Bhumi 81
visas 104
Viya 100

W
walking 105
Wasabi 64, 77
water safety 109
weather 104
websites 106
Weights and measures 107
White Tiger (Adiga) 58
Willingdon, Lady 24
Woh Chokri (film) 59
women travellers 109
wrestling 12

Y
Yamuna River 81
YMCA 114
The Yum Yum Tree 67, 99

Z
Zafar II, Bahadur Shah (emperor) 37, 49, 81
Zafar Mahal 8, 21, 45
Zaffran 98
Zamani, Mariam 33
Zamin, Imam 19
zardozi 62
Zaza 100
Zinat ul Nisa 53, 82
Zinat ul Masjid 45, 53, 82

# Acknowledgments

### The Authors

Gavin Thomas is a London-based travel writer specializing in the Gulf, Sri Lanka and, especially, India. He is the author of the *The Rough Guide to Dubai*, *The Rough Guide to Sri Lanka*, co-author of *The Rough Guide to Rajasthan, Delhi and Agra* and a contributing author to *The Rough Guide to India*.

Janice Pariat is a freelance writer based in Shillong. She has lived and worked in Delhi for almost a decade and loves the city's clash of culture, pace and climate. She writes travel stories for *HT City* (Mumbai) and *Travel to Care*, a website dedicated to eco-tourism.

**Photographer** Idris Ahmed
**Additional Photography** Idris Ahmed; Andy Crawford; Christopher and Sally Gable; Frank Grace; Dinesh Khanna; Dave King; Bobby Kohli; Diya Kohli; Amit Pasricha; Aditya Patankar; Christopher Pillitz; Ram Rahman; Rough Guides: Simon Bracken, Shruti Singhi; B.P.S. Walia.
**Fact Checker** Aparajita Kumar

### At DK INDIA

**Managing Editor** Aruna Ghose
**Senior Editorial Manager** Savitha Kumar
**Senior Design Manager** Priyanka Thakur
**Project Editor** Trisha Bora
**Project Designer** Shruti Singhi
**Assistant Cartographic Manager** Suresh Kumar
**Cartographer** Jasneet Kaur
**Senior Picture Research Coordinator** Taiyaba Khatoon
**DTP Coordinator** Azeem Siddiqui
**Indexer** Cyber Media Services Ltd.

### At DK LONDON

**Publisher** Douglas Amrine
**List Manager** Julie Oughton
**Design Manager** Mabel Chan
**Senior Editor** Sadie Smith
**Designer** Tracy Smith
**Cartographer** Stuart James
**DTP Operator** Jason Little
**Production Controller** Rebecca Short

### Picture Credits

t=top; tc=top centre; tr=top right; cla=centre left above; ca=centre above; cra=centre right above; cl=centre left; c=centre; cr=centre right; clb=centre left below; cb=centre below; crb=centre right below; bl=bottom left; bc=bottom centre; br=bottom right; ftl=far top left; ftr=far top right; fcla=far centre left above; fcra=far centre right above; fcl=far centre left; fcr=far centre right; fclb=far centre left below; fcrb=far centre right below; fbl=far bottom left; fbr=far bottom right.

Every effort has been made to trace the copyright holders, and we apologize in advance for any unintentional omissions. We would be pleased to insert the appropriate acknowledgments in any subsequent edition of this publication.

### Photography Permissions

Dorling Kindersley would like to thank the following for their assistance and kind permission to photograph at their establishments: Rakesh Thakore at Abraham & Thakore, Amrapali, K. D. Singh at The Bookshop, Mushtak Khan at Crafts Museum, Gandhi Smriti, Dhiraj Srivastava at Indira Gandhi Memorial Museum, Anil Pershad at Lala Chunna Mal's Haveli, Rajeev Lochan at National Gallery of Modern Art, K. K. S. Deori & S. K. Pathak at National Museum, Mayank Tiwari at National

Rail Museum, Mridula Mukherjee at Nehru Memorial Museum and Library, Ogaan Closet, Ravissant, Kabir Singh at The Shop and Anita Jha and Pratibha Raman at Sulabh International Museum of Toilets.

The publisher would like to thank the following individuals, companies, and picture libraries for their kind permission to reproduce their photographs:

4CORNERS IMAGES: SIME/ Giampiccolo Angelo 3br,/ HP Huber 34-35.
IDRIS AHMED: 3bl, 6bc, 14-15c, 17cb, 25clb.
AKG-IMAGES: Yvan Travert 43tr.
ALAMY IMAGES: Bill Bachmann 6cr; Dinodia Images 89b; Ulana Switucha 24c.
AMARYA HAVELI: 112tl.
THE ASHOKA, DELHI: 66bl.
ATLANTIC BOOKS: *The White Tiger*, published by Atlantic Books, jacket design by Gray318 58ca.
B NINETEEN: 116tl.
CASA BOUTIQUE HOTELS: 116tr.
CHOR BIZARRE: 85tl.
CORBIS: Jan Butchofsky-Houser 4-5; Jim Zuckerman 95bl.
GINGER HOTELS: 114tr.
HIS GRACE B&B: 118tl.
HOTEL BROADWAY: 115tl.
HOTEL PALACE HEIGHTS: 112tr, 115tc.
HYATT REGENCY DELHI: 98tr, 99tc, 101t.

THE IMPERIAL: 65tl, 65tr, 117tc.
ITC MAURYA: Bukhara 64tl, 93tl.
LEGENDS OF INDIA: 77tc, 113tl.
THE MANOR: 98tl.
MARY EVANS PICTURE LIBRARY: 36tc.
NATIONAL SCHOOL OF DRAMA: 50b.
NEW DELHI YMCA: 114tl.
OBEROI HOTELS & RESORTS: 64tr, 67tl, 117tl, 119tl.
THE PARK NEW DELHI: 66tl, 79tl, 79tr.
AMIT PASRICHA: 60t.
PENGUIN BOOKS LTD: 58tl, 58tc, 58tr, 59bl.
PHOTOLIBRARY: Akhil Bakshi 40b; Walter Bibikow: 102-103; Bilderbuch 80tl; David Davis 30-31c; Klaus Lang 70-71; Mary Evans Picture Library 36bc; G & R Maschmeyer 86-87; Marcus Oleniuk 2tr; Pietro Scozzari 1c; Eitan Simanor 80cl; The British Library 37tl.
SANGEET NATAK AKADEMI: 50tl.
THE TAJ MAHAL HOTEL, NEW DELHI: 64br, 65br, 66tr, 67tr, 77tl, 113tr.
VANDANA'S B&B: 118tr.
VIYA HOME: 100tc.
THE YUM YUM TREE: 99tl.
All other images © Dorling Kindersley
For further information see:
*www.dkimages.com*

## Special Editions of DK Travel Guides

# Selected Street Index

| | | | |
|---|---|---|---|
| Africa Avenue | U1 | Hindu Rao Marg | F1 |
| Ajmal Khan Road | D3 | Hoshiar Singh Marg | E3 |
| Ajmeri Gate Road | G4 | Humayun Road | P4 |
| Akbar Road | N4 | Idgah Road | E3 |
| Alaknanda Badarpur Road | W3 | Indraprastha Marg | J7 |
| Alipur Road | G1 | Jai Singh Marg | N1 |
| Amrita Shergill Marg | P5 | Janpath | N3 |
| Anuvrat Marg | U3 | Jantar Mantar Road | N2 |
| Arab ki Sarai Road | S6 | Jaswant Singh Road | P2 |
| Aruna Asaf Ali Marg | U2 | Jawaharlal Nehru Marg | G5 |
| Arya School Lane | E7 | Jawaharlal Nehru Stadium | |
| Asaf Ali Road | H5 | Marg | Q7 |
| Ashok Road | N2 | Jhandewalan Road | E4 |
| Atul Grove Road | P1 | Jor Bagh Road | P7 |
| August Kranti Marg | V1 | Josip Broz Tito Marg | W2 |
| Aurangzeb Road | N5 | Kachehri Road | F2 |
| Aurobindo Marg | V2 | Kali Bari Road | D7 |
| Azad Market Road | E2 | Kalindi Kunj Road | Y2 |
| Baba Ganganath Marg | U2 | Kamal Ataturk Marg | M6 |
| Baba Kharak Singh Marg | E7 | Kamaraj Road | M4 |
| Bahadur Shah Zafar Marg | H6 | Karta Nawab Gali | G3 |
| Bahadurgarh Road | E2 | Kasabpur Road | E4 |
| Ballimaran | G3 | Kasturba Gandhi Marg | P2 |
| Bangla Sahib Road | E7 | Kasturba Hospital Marg | H4 |
| Bara Hindu Rao Road | E3 | Katra Bariyan | F3 |
| Barakhamba Road | P1 | Kautilya Marg | L5 |
| Basant Road | F5 | Khari Baoli Road | F3 |
| Bazaar Chitli Qabar Marg | H5 | Khel Gaon Marg | V2 |
| Bhagwan Das Road | Q2 | Khirki Main Road | V2 |
| Bhai Vir Singh Marg | E7 | Kotla Marg | H6 |
| Bhairon Marg | R3 | Kripa Narayan Marg | G1 |
| Bharat Scouts & | | Krishna Menon Marg | M4 |
| Guides Marg | R6 | Lal Bahadur Shastri Road | R6 |
| Bhav Bhutti Marg | G5 | Lala Hardev Sahai Marg | G1 |
| Bhisham Pitamah Marg | P6 | Lala Lajpat Rai Path | R7 |
| Birbal Road | R7 | Lalkuan Bazaar Road | G4 |
| Brassey Avenue | L3 | Lambi Gali | G4 |
| Canning Road | P2 | Lawrence Road | L1 |
| Central Golf Link Road | Q6 | Liberty Road | E2 |
| Ch Brahan Prakash Marg | F1 | Link Road | D5 |
| Chamelian Road | E3 | Lodi Road | P6 |
| Chandni Chowk | G3 | Lok Sabha Marg | M2 |
| Chandragupta Marg | K5 | Maharaja Aggarsain Marg | F3 |
| Chawri Bazaar Road | G4 | Maharaja Ranjeet | |
| Chel Puri | G4 | Singh Marg | G6 |
| Chelmsford Road | F6 | Maharishi Balmiki Marg | E3 |
| Church Mission Marg | G3 | Maharishi Raman Marg | P5 |
| Church Road | L2 | Mahatma Gandhi Marg | S5 |
| Churi Walan Gali | G4 | Mahatma Jyoti Rao | |
| Connaught Circus | F7 | Phule Road | Q2 |
| Copernicus Marg | Q2 | Main Bazaar Road | E5 |
| Dalhousie Road | M3 | Man Singh Road | P3 |
| Dariba Kalan Road | H3 | Mathura Road | R4 |
| Daulat Ram Marg | F3 | Maulana Azad Road | N3 |
| DCM Road | D2 | Maulana Mohammad | |
| Deen Dayal Upadhyaya | | Ali Marg | X2 |
| Marg | H6 | Max Mueller Marg | P6 |
| Desh Bandhu Gupta Road | F5 | Meena Bazaar | H4 |
| Dr Bishambar Das Marg | M1 | Mehrauli Badarpur Road | W3 |
| Dr Rajendra Prasad Road | N2 | Mirdard Marg | H6 |
| Dr Zakir Hussain Marg | Q4 | Moolchand Flyover | W1 |
| Dupleix Marg | M4 | More Sarai Road | H3 |
| Eastern Avenue | X1 | Mother Teresa Crescent | K2 |
| Esplanade Road | H4 | Motilal Nehru Marg | N4 |
| Feroz Shah Road | P2 | Nai Sarak | G4 |
| Gali Halwai Wali | F6 | Nauroji Nagar Marg | U1 |
| Geetanjali Marg | V2 | Nawab Road | E3 |
| Grand Trunk Road | E1 | Naya Bans Bazaar | F3 |
| Guru Ravi Das Marg | X3 | Naya Bazaar | F3 |
| Gurudwara Rakab | | Nelson Mandela Marg | T2 |
| Ganj Road | M2 | Netaji Subhash Marg | H4 |
| Hailey Road | G7 | New Rohtak Road | D3 |
| Hamilton Road | G2 | Nicholson Road | G2 |
| Hanuman Road | N1 | Niti Marg | L6 |
| Nityanand Marg | F2 | | |
| Noida Toll Bridge | X1 | | |
| North Avenue | L2 | | |
| Nyaya Marg | K6 | | |
| Outer Ring Road | X2 | | |
| Panchkuian Road | E5 | | |
| Panchsheel Marg | K5 | | |
| Pandara Road | Q4 | | |
| Pandit Pant Marg | M1 | | |
| Park Street | L1 | | |
| Poorvi Marg | T2 | | |
| Press Enclave Marg | V3 | | |
| Prithviraj Lane | P5 | | |
| Prithviraj Road | N5 | | |
| Purana Qila Road | Q3 | | |
| Qutab Road | F3 | | |
| Race Course Road | M5 | | |
| Rafi Ahmed Kidwai Marg | N3 | | |
| Raisina Hill | M3 | | |
| Raisina Road | N2 | | |
| Raj Niwas Marg | F1 | | |
| Raja Dhirsain Marg | W2 | | |
| Rajaji Marg | M4 | | |
| Rajesh Pilot Marg | N5 | | |
| Rajpath | N3 | | |
| Rajya Sabha Marg | M2 | | |
| Ram Bagh Road | D2 | | |
| Rama Krishna Ashram Marg | L1 | | |
| Rani Jhansi Road | E3 | | |
| Rao Tula Ram Marg | T1 | | |
| Ring Road | S4 | | |
| Road No 13 A | Y2 | | |
| Roshanara Road | E1 | | |
| Safdarjung Road | M5 | | |
| Sansad Marg | M2 | | |
| Sardar Patel Marg | K4 | | |
| Satya Marg | K7 | | |
| Satya Sadan | L7 | | |
| Second Avenue | N7 | | |
| Shaheed Bhagat Singh | | | |
| Marg | E6 | | |
| Shaheed Jeet Singh Marg | U2 | | |
| Shahjahan Road | P4 | | |
| Sham Nath Marg | G2 | | |
| Shanti Path | K6 | | |
| Shersham Road | Q3 | | |
| Shraddhanand Marg | F4 | | |
| Shyama Prasad Mukherji | | | |
| Marg | G3 | | |
| Sikandra Road | Q1 | | |
| Siri Fort Marg | V2 | | |
| Sitaram Bazaar Road | G4 | | |
| South Avenue | L4 | | |
| Subramaniam Bharti Marg | P5 | | |
| Swarna Jayanti Marg | T1 | | |
| Talkatora Road | M2 | | |
| Tambraparini Marg | R3 | | |
| Tansen Marg | G7 | | |
| Teen Murti Marg | M5 | | |
| Tees January Marg | N5 | | |
| Thyagaraja Marg | M4 | | |
| Tilak Bazaar | F3 | | |
| Tilak Marg | Q2 | | |
| Tolstoy Marg | N1 | | |
| Tughlaq Road | N5 | | |
| Turkman Marg | G6 | | |
| V Desika Mandir Marg | U2 | | |
| Vandemataram Marg | D5 | | |
| Vasant Marg | T1 | | |
| Vekanand Road (Minto Rd) | G5 | | |
| Vijay Chowk | M3 | | |
| Vikas Marg | J7 | | |
| Vinay Marg | L7 | | |
| Zorawar Singh Marg | F2 | | |

Selected Street Index